From Hood to Headship

A Black woman's journey to becoming
a headteacher

C000165849

Miriam Manderson

Published by

Peaches

Publications

Published in London by Peaches Publications Ltd, 2022.

www.peachespublications.co.uk

The moral right of the author has been asserted.

Images courtesy of iStock Getty & Free Pik.

British Library Cataloguing in Publication Data: A catalogue record for this book is available from the British Library.

ISBN: 9798835649174

Book cover design: Peaches Publications and Miriam Manderson

Editor: Linda Green

Typesetter: Winsome Duncan

Proofreader: Virginia Rounding

Disclaimer

This book is a memoir and reflects the author's present recollections of experiences over a period of time. Names and characteristics have been changed to protect the identity and preserve the dignity of the individuals. Some events have been paraphrased based on recollections, and some selected dialogue has been recreated or adapted.

The views and opinions expressed in *From Hood to Headship* are those of the author and are not necessarily those of the publisher, editor or any other third parties. Any content provided by the author is of their opinion, and is not intended to malign any religion, cultural or ethnic group, club, organisation, company, individual or anyone or anything. The designations employed in this publication and the presentation of material therein do not imply the expression of any opinion whatsoever on the part of any other parties concerning the legal status of any country or area or concerning the demarcation of its boundaries.

Table of Contents

Dedication

This book is dedicated to the memory of my beloved and late mother, Mrs Esther Blankson, who I know is looking down on me proudly, and to my father, Mr George 'Jubilee' Blankson, who has always said to me: 'Be bold.'

Thank you both for bringing me into this world to touch and inspire others through education.

From Hood to Headship

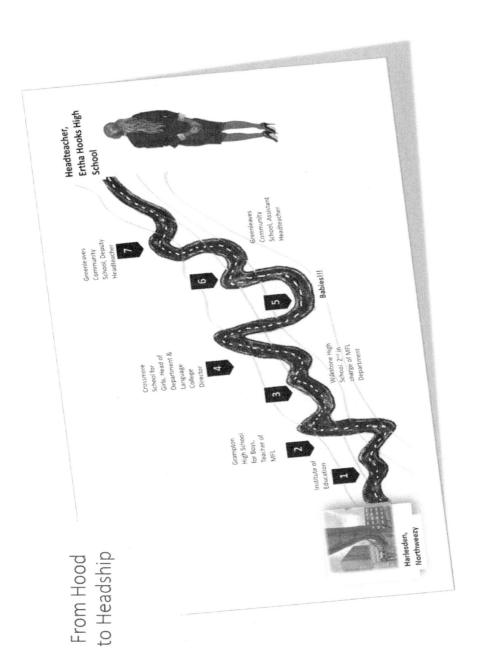

Headteacher, Ertha Hooks High School

Greenleaves Community School, Deputy Headteacher

Greenleaves Community School, Assistant Headteacher

Crossmere School for Girls, Head of Department & Language College Director

Wilkstone High School, 2nd in charge of MFL Department

Babies!!!

Grampton High School for Boys, Teacher of MFL

Institute of Education

Harlesden, Northweezy

'Our deepest fear is not that we are inadequate. Our deepest fear is that we are powerful beyond measure.'

(Marianne Williamson 2015)

£5:50

Order Placed
June 13, 2022.
Delivered
June 15, 2022,
John. 13:15ᴮ
Serve Each Other
just as I Served You.
Easy-to-Read Version.

O Master let me Walk
With Thee

In lowly paths of
Service free.
Washington Gladden.

Acknowledgements

Today I recognise my awesomeness and the strength behind the spirit of those who guide me.

Islands are to be inhabited. No one lives their life alone. No one achieves for themselves alone. No one ever went far alone. In fact, there is an African saying that states: 'If you want to go fast, go alone. If you want to go far, go together.' There is always someone rooting for you. You just need to seek and find them. It is for this reason that this page is dedicated to those mentors, guardian angels, spirits both living and some who are no longer on this earth with us but who have all in some way touched my journey. I am lucky to be surrounded by many and recognise them all. There would be too many to mention, but for this first publication I have pulled together my list of champions. Everyone needs a champion. Thank you to mine: Ms Nichols, Ms Simmonds, Madame Nouqueret, Tom Buzzard, Sherry Davis, Jan Cartwright, Bernie Peploe, Denise Fox, Phil Egan, Maggie Rafee, Paulette Minott-Statham, Andria Zafirakou MBE, Candise Lazare, Howard Freed, Dr John Reavley, Dad – Mr George Blankson, bro – John Blankson, sis – Julia Blankson, hubby – Theo Manderson. Each one of you has played a role as a champion in my life and some of you continue to do so. I also owe a huge debt of gratitude to my supporters on all my social media platforms who wanted to see this book published and many who contributed to my Go Fund Me page. You are all awesome and some of you get double thanks if you are mentioned separately here – so, well done you!

This book has been influenced by two individuals: Howard Freed and Dr John Reavley. Howard, you don't know how much being a 'guardian angel' has been a part of my journey in leadership. All it takes is a few words from a 'leadership god' and you're inspired. That person was you. Dr John Reavley has unreservedly demonstrated how to successfully, confidently and deliberately pass on the mantle. A person of true confidence and humility who does not boast, despite having over 30 years of leadership experience.

My deepest appreciation to:

My new-found soul sister, Neusa Catoja, who inspired me to 'just do this' from her book launch. If it were not for you launching your book and taking the time to allow me to be one of your invited guests, this book would not have materialised. Thank you for not only providing this platform but becoming a sister-friend who has now become part of my personal journey.

My School Holidays WhatsApp group, you have no idea how much our WhatsApp chats keep me sane, help me stay in touch with the real world, and blow my mind: Cleo, Aunty Jacquie and Shirley, (my Zumba Queens), Dr Michele C. McDowell, Saffron, Shaleen and their sister Shareen, the 'relative' to my leadership sister, Candise, who is part of the leadership sisterhood 'Thor's Whores' with Andria Zafirakou (MBE) or Zaff as I like to fondly call her, and Aunty P (aka Paulette Minott-Statham) always saying she is 'proud' of me at every stage. My beloved sister, Julia, who is as crazy as they come but has this ability to just 'know' when I need her and when to stop me from running myself into the ground, building the resilience needed. My husband, Theo Manderson, you are simply awesome. You know when they say, behind every good man there is a woman? Well, thank you for highlighting the reverse, for being the man behind me, in front of me, around me when I have needed that extra support, confidence-building, and champion at home. Your belief in me being able to accomplish anything is not only unconditional but also perpetual. My sons, Rahsaan – who we fondly renamed Jazz – and Isaiah: thank you for listening to mummy read you parts of this and acting as my mini-editors. You demonstrated such maturity in your understanding of leadership dilemmas and I hope seeing me on this journey inspires you to be leaders of your own lives.

To my editor, Linda Green, thank you for your wisdom and the laughter we shared as we worked together. Thanks too to my proofreader, Virginia Rounding. Winsome Duncan, I am so thankful for your determination to see others succeed. Your passion, permission and pushing others to excel is the secret ingredient of your success. Thank you for allowing me to get to the finished product. I know it is not your name, but I love calling you 'Peaches' – you embody your publishing company.

I would like to acknowledge Audiomotion for the 'Which Step Have You Reached Today?' video, (found at: https://www.youtube.com/watch?v=m4hKFpuxEOM) which inspired me and is used in this book.

Foreword

It is with a heart bursting with pride to have the opportunity of writing the foreword to my dear friend Miriam's long-awaited debut book *From Hood to Headship*. I have always been in awe of this woman and in these few words I would like to share with you why.

I have known Miriam for more than 13 years, initially as a work colleague where I adopted her as my secret mentor, but now where she plays the role of a dear friend and member of my big fat extended family.

We first met in 2008 when she had recently been appointed as the new assistant headteacher in my school. At that time, the school was on a challenging journey and the headteacher wanted to grow and enhance a new leadership team who would support their vision; hence Miriam was the perfect candidate to help make this happen.

My first impressions of meeting this smartly dressed and stylish woman who could glide like a swan on her three-inch heels and who would mesmerise you with her most extraordinary hairstyles, was a football world cup shout-out 'yessssss!', that I had found somebody, another woman I could connect with and who was funny, strong and kind but, most importantly, who would be an inspiring role model to our students, our staff and to myself. Indeed, Miriam could communicate and connect with everyone and would make them feel valued and important, regardless of their knowledge and background. It is fair to say that it is impossible not to gravitate towards her and be influenced and to follow.

As a result, I have learnt so much from my dear friend Miriam, particularly over the last five years where I witnessed her long and tough journey in finally getting her well-deserved school headship position.

During this period the learning which took place for me was invaluable and quite often painful, especially as I felt helpless for her. She encountered many obstacles, conversations were tough, and opportunities for headship positions were few and far between, all of which will be shared with us later in this book. I would often reflect and ask myself whether Miriam is secretly wearing a Teflon non-stick outfit underneath her suit, with the aim of rejecting negative thoughts and sadness, as you would never have guessed the ongoing challenges she was dealing with. However, my greatest learning from Miriam is that, when you want something so desperately and you share this message to the universe, it will happen and there are always people willing to help you get there if you are brave enough to ask.

Miriam has written this book not as a trophy of her success in becoming a headteacher which has always been a lifelong ambition for her, but mostly as a guidebook or source of inspiration to help others who are on similar journeys and who need to see what resilience, inner strength and self-belief can achieve.

In life, we know there are continuous blockers and a lack of opportunities, especially for women and even more so for women of colour. This book will help us to see that labels and socioeconomic status do not define us; instead, it is our attitudes to all communities, kindness and service to others that do. As Michelle Obama beautifully stated in her address to the Democratic National Convention in July 2016, 'When they go low, we go high.' Please now sit back and enjoy reading how Miriam demonstrates to us all how this is achieved.

Andria Zafirakou MBE
Global Teacher Prize Winner 2018

This is a book full of warmth, humour and courage. So intimately written that the reader cannot help but find themselves drawn into Miriam's life and the unfolding of her story. And what an amazing story it is! The story of a 'London-born UK-Black West African child' who overcame a plethora of obstacles to achieve her dream of becoming a headteacher. This book is a must-read, particularly for aspiring leaders of colour. Miriam's words will inspire and motivate and show you that, even in the face of adversity, it is possible to achieve your dreams.

Viv Grant
Director, Integrity Coaching

Preface

'If you think it, you gotta ink it.'
(Mark Victor Hansen, n.d.)

If I was given a pound for every time somebody asked me, 'How do you do it?' 'How do you balance all that you do?' 'How are you so efficient and successful at everything you do?' I would be very rich indeed and I would have a real reason to be writing a book and counting on my fame. I want to share how an ordinary person achieves, not extraordinary things, but successes through others. There is an overarching theme with this perspective too: that I am a Black woman.

Did you know that in 2018 there were over 22,000 headteachers for primary and secondary in the UK? Did you know that 15,000 headteachers were female? Did you know that 0.7% of the 22,000 headteachers were of Black origin, with 0.2% of Black African origin? Did you know that there were approximately 40 Black male headteachers, 10 of those being heads of secondary schools? Finally, do you realise that I make up 1 of the 0.2% of the 22,000 headteachers of Black African and female grouping in the UK?

The first Black headteacher in Britain was Yvonne Conolly who, sadly, passed away in January 2021. Fifty-one years later, *From Hood to Headship* takes us on an impassioned journey to see the view from my humble beginnings in inner-city London, through the eyes of a London-born UK-Black West African child, and provides one perspective of what it takes to become one of Britain's very few Black headteachers. There should be many more like me by now.

If we lack support and the existence of those who give us agency, then there will always be a mountain of untapped potential sitting amongst and within the Black community. The idea of privilege is real. The institutional racism that has made disadvantage a persistent problem amongst certain communities means that, at the grassroots level, some accept the status quo.

The answer in my view is overcoming our challenges, the negative traumas from our history, infiltrating as best we can the organisations and positions of leadership so that we can create change. In my role as a headteacher, I believe I am among those in society who can influence and create change.

The late Stephen Covey, author of *The 7 Habits of Highly Successful People* (Covey, 1989), suggests we should write ourselves a personal mission statement. Many other authors have written about this in similar ways, often talking about how we should attach a mantra to ourselves, defining a 'mantra' as an inspiring principle we glue to ourselves and live by at all times. Loving this idea, I decided to give myself two main mantras.

The first is: 'everything she touched turned to good'. I want to be like King Midas, someone who always converts whatever they do into something 'gold' which is always associated with something special, wealth. Wealth can be of different sources: family wealth, health wealth, friendship wealth, the wealth of wisdom, and of course monetary wealth. I couldn't keep the same saying – 'everything she touched turned to gold' – so as a teacher, I thought about the Ofsted criteria and, though I don't want to use 'outstanding', I thought 'good' sounded just as 'good as gold', if you get what I mean.

The second mantra I walk in is to 'live to leave a legacy'. Leaving a legacy means you can have people who carry on the good work that you have put in place, using in turn their generated wealth to share the goodness with others. In this book, I'm sharing my humble experiences in the hope that others can be aroused to use their wealth of experiences to their advantage. In my job every day I intend to touch and inspire my children through good leadership and turn them into society's wealth, creating a legacy of upstanding and responsible, compassionate, educated and free-speaking individuals.

Who am I? More importantly, who am I to be writing this book? Well, I figured that all this journaling I've been doing must count for something. I wanted to put my days down on paper. I'm not somebody famous; I'm not a writer; I'm not an actor; I'm not the world's best teacher or headteacher; I'm not somebody who has become famous due to some huge pressure of adversity or acts of philanthropy, or a saviour through a disaster-stricken or terror-ridden event. I'm just simply an ordinary citizen of London who happens to be a headteacher who happens to want to share their story on paper. I do, however, recognise that I stand on some very solid shoulders of individuals who have paved the way to allow someone like me to rise to the position of headteacher; a member of a considered group of people who are society's guardians of foundational principles and important societal values. So much so that we too live and work by the seven principles of public life, also known as the Nolan Principles: selflessness, integrity, objectivity, accountability, openness, honesty and leadership.

Amongst those shoulders are those from Black and other ethnic groups. I dislike the term BAME, especially the reference to minority, recognising that in the world we are not that. When I travel to Ghana, my country of heritage, the phrase 'ethnic minority' is defunct. It isn't even used in reference to those of Caucasian ethnicity who live in the country. I recognise the importance of my seat at the table and feel it is important that I use this space to record my experiences, especially when in 2020 the UCL Institute of Education (IoE) journal published a new study which found that 46% of all schools in England have no Black, Asian or other ethnic groups as leaders and that there is an underrepresentation of senior leaders in leadership teams from the same groups of people (UCL, 2020).

So I hope that you enjoy reading my chronicle.

If anything, perhaps it will be at least a tiny bit of inspiration to others, a sense of hope, a sense of overcoming challenges and an understanding of how women like me can 'do it', whatever 'it' may be – in my case, to reach one of the highest echelons in education, a headteacher, despite adversity. After all, balloons will rise given the right conditions, irrespective of what colour they are.

I have always 'journaled', feeling it was a safe place, if not the safest place, to write my thoughts and reflections. This includes highs, lows, frustrations, challenges and complex situations that I have needed to work through.

After years of journaling in several types of spaces and books, including blogs, online diaries and beautifully decorated journals, it was time for me to design one which blended both the professional and personal aspects of life and, in particular, my career stage.

The life of a senior leader can be hectic. You are also caught between having many expectations of you from both above and below, without the recourse of being able to show signs of weakness for fear of reducing the confidence and faith others have in you to do your role. A duty of care is always exercised towards the staff. The Chair of Governors looks after the headteacher but who looks after the senior leaders?

The senior leader also holds a very private space. No one quite knows what is really going on in the mind of the leader as they navigate situations each day. It is important to get out of their heads all the thoughts they have, so they can take a step back and look at the reality of themselves. It can help to change or even improve perspectives. It can help in making decisions, of which there are many, and it can help with retaining and sustaining the confidence required.

Capturing my feelings and reflecting along the way was therapy for me. Self-created quiet time to just stew in the eventualities of a massive part of my life – work. There is a saying that you should not live to work, but work to live. On many occasions, I definitely have had the first part of this saying actively working in my life. I have dedicated much time trying to find the antidote and swinging the balance in favour of the second part of the saying, with partial success. I continue to search for the key.

We can surmise that life is about balance – balance according to what *we* feel gives us balance, and that is not always a 50/50 balance, but that in which we find an equilibrium that works for us and gives us a sense of inner peace and satisfaction.

So, when you get to the core of my story, the part when I apply for headship posts, you will find this interjected with a series of my journal reflections to really capture you in my thinking at the time. I wanted you to get inside my head, maybe nod in empathy or raise your eyebrows in surprise or even grow to understand what happens during times such as these, for those of us who appear to have ourselves sorted.

I chose to tell my tale, not as a show of ego or stating 'look how well I have done', but in the hope that a normal person like me can share insights into my experiences in a way that might help, support and, dare I say, inspire someone else. Yes, there may be times when I relish my success. I am not boasting but showcasing, as I am not alone in this arena. Being ordinary has its advantages, in that others can relate to and see themselves in you.

There is a feeling of solidarity, a kind of 'we are all in this together' type of adage, that is worn like a banner and, in a sort of secretly woven silken thread, binds those of us who are leaders, together. As you read my stories contributing to my journey, I hope that you will find tales that you may empathise with, laugh or even cry with. One thing about this for certain is that it will demonstrate you are not alone in the world of leadership and the challenges it brings. I hope that, somehow, anyone who reads this gets something that meets their need, be it to educate, inspire, question or clarify.

You know that feeling we get when we release dopamine into our bodies? Well, journaling acts as my set of dopamine injections. This book came about as a development of my thinking as I created a leader's journal which was the beginning of my writing juncture and within which you will also find parts of this very preface. If you do use a journal as I do, enjoy the journey and, after a year, review it to see just how phenomenal you are as a leader. My journal has now become this book. It offers only one individual's outlook, because I know there are many perspectives out there.

Each of us has a unique voice. This is mine.

A friend once said to me,

'Leadership is what it is all about and, although the role carries many responsibilities and we deal with weighty issues, we don't have to wear them heavily.'

'Today is the first day of your 365-page novel. Write a good one!'

(Brad Paisley, 2010)

Part 1

Beginnings: the girl from the 'hood'

1. North Weezy

'Black is growin' up around your family and makin' it
Then being forced to leave the place you love because
there's hate in it
People say you fake the shit, never stayed to change the shit
But black is bein jealous, youd be dead if you had stayed in it'
(Dave, 2019)

Harlesden – possibly one of the most iconic epicentres of UK Black Caribbean culture in London. Definitely, a place you could say hosted the best of Jamaican and British UK reggae music, with the host of reggae singers who either lived or had an association with the place. Not to mention the home of Starlight, BodyMusic and the classic Hawkeye music record shops. (Yes, I did say 'record' – remember those?) Neighboured by Willesden, Neasden, Church Road and Church End Estate, the latter two so large they warrant being towns in themselves, though they span across from Harlesden, Willesden and Stonebridge to the west, and Acton and Kensal Rise to the south and west. I was born in Park Royal Hospital in the early seventies. Well, I believe its official name is the Central Middlesex Hospital, but Park Royal is where it sits. We all were born there, my cousins, brother and sister, and I. Sitting on the cusp of Acton and Harlesden in northwest London. My memorable journey began in Neasden, NW2, but swiftly moved to the Stonebridge estate. On the ninth out of 15 floors of the high-rise Prothero House. I would run crazy through the buildings which all linked together on alternate landings. It was a criminal's haven if you wanted to run away from the police, or any other person giving chase. The word 'safeguarding' could never have existed then as the size of the windows on each balcony were large enough for five people to jump through and instantly commit suicide. It did happen once or twice during the time I lived there, but I am amazed I don't have many stories to tell about that. Phew!

The area is dominated by the postcodes NW10 and NW2 and is proudly referenced by some as 'North Weezy'. Harlesden was by far the 'capital' of North Weezy, a town full of residential houses, streets lined with multiple cash and carry shops, several versions of Black hair product shops, predominantly Asian-owned, Caribbean record and food shops and versions of fake KFCs, in addition to the one real KFC shop: the only one I know of in London that stayed open beyond 3:00 a.m. every weekend and cooked its chicken right through so you could see no blood. It cooked the best hot wings.

Walk down the main Harlesden High Street on any day and you would be guaranteed to smell delightful smells of Caribbean food, hear the sounds of reggae music and bump into all the people you know, making your 10-minute pop to the shops take longer than an hour. Add some sunshine and you would absolutely be entertained by batty riders, a rainbow of colourful hairstyles and vibrant voices. Youths on bikes, some doing errands for their mums, others simply out with their friends. You might catch a whiff of weed – marijuana – but you would be hard-pressed to work out from where it originated. That would be unless of course, like me, you had grown up there and could recognise the young man who had just passed you with his melancholy smile and red eyes – or knew of the so-called 'weed houses' – or caught a glimpse of the car whose driver, window down and music blasting, held a 'spliff' in his hand as he watched and admired the derrières of the best of Harlesden's young women, suitably clad in sexy outfits, sporting immaculately done nails, probably from one of the many nail shops, and wearing a weave or boasting an elaborate coiffure, whether a weave, relaxed or beautiful extension plaits.

Occasionally, too, you would savour the sounds of someone's music from their blasting Jammo speakers or a celebration of some sort taking place in a house party. In our childhood, we spent our time playing out a lot.

Estate children benefit from the joy of having everyone's windows looking in on the areas where the kids hang out. There was Marlo's mother, who at 8:00 p.m. every evening chimed out in her thick Bajan (Barbadian) accent: 'Marlo, come and get your dinner now!'

He would bow his head in shame and sprint to his block in the hope that we would not get to see his mother actually step out to holler at him again, should he not arrive at the door by her intuitive mother timer.

Then there was Denton, who always played his music loud enough for us to hear from his bedroom window, no matter where we were on the estate. Nobody complained. Some of the older kids would congregate at the bottom and listen to the thumping bass line and even dance – a free rave or party.

There was the occasional arrival of other kids from other areas who always wanted to join the groups on our estate. They would come and go, recognising they were not the 'original' crew. A characteristic typical of many areas.

What didn't exist was this ridiculous 'ends' mentality which means nowadays youths cannot travel to parts they don't live in, for fear of being accosted, troubled, or even sadly harmed by someone claiming rights to their life, just because they are not from that neck of the woods. Utter nonsense, which I am led to believe is derived from the UK's cousin, the USA's 'Bloods and Crips wars', transferred to the predominantly deprived areas of London.

What the youth of today don't realise is ownership of land in the USA is exactly that: ownership of large parts of land, shops, businesses, trade, some offering an alternative type of safety in exchange for another good or service. Unlike what the UK 'cousins' try to emulate which leads only to sheer mindless stabbing or harming of another, with no giving back to the community at large. This is only a small part of a very complex issue which I am not qualified to judge or make a point of in this book.

Then, there was my dad, the very regal but majestic speaker, whose accent and African-laced tone demanded authority and respect. Dad derives from a legacy of high achievers, going as far back as our Ghanaian Fante King. So, as he would often tell me, we were princesses, of royalty, and we should always expect to meet the highest expectations. Woe betide anyone who spoke to dad disrespectfully; in fact, no one did. Simply because he oozed royalty and authority. Dad had an air about him that commanded fairness, no nonsense, strictness, but at the same time a fierceness and gentleness all combined into one. His intolerance of a degenerate culture of being a layabout, lack of ambition, and disregard for education was always made very clear.

His deep passion for Christianity was demonstrated every Sunday as he joined in the natural musical festival of Stonebridge or Church Road, wherever we stayed, by blasting out his version of 'tunes' out of the front-room window – Jim Reeves being one of the most audible. As you can see, music was very much an intrinsic part of the culture and atmosphere of northwest London and, to this day, there is an incredible but cohesive tolerance by the authorities of the music and ambience created that is rare to see in other parts of London.

Dad would be clear about the time we needed to be home from the adventure playground, staggering times according to the ages of my sister, brother, and me. I was the one he expected home first but I never made it, covering myself by stating I was with my four-year older brother, roller skating around. However, if necessary, dad would not hesitate to come onto the balcony of the said community estate and very loudly and embarrassingly call us home.

I remember one day trying to beat dad as I saw him in slow motion open the door, look left and right, not see me – although I could see him – and proceed to leave his home to come and find me. Staying out late on this occasion was not a good idea. As I began to race home, I took one extended stride, launching my leg forward. I slipped and fell into the splits, delaying my 'race against dad' and as I leapt up and ran as fast as I could, with my heart thumping in my chest, I could hear the belly laughter of the friend I left behind rolling around in absolute hysterics. To this day, a whole 35 years on, the recollection of this still has us laughing in absolute stitches. I made it home though, just before him and just in time so that I am alive to tell this tale. Let's just say, the fear of dad was upon me and I had to act swiftly.

African dads are not to be messed about with.

Strict is a euphemism for how dad brought us up, and this is me, the youngest, saying this. As we all know, with the last born, parents usually ease up a bit, so you can only imagine how he was with children numbers one and two. My brother today, being a child genius with nothing less than grade A for all his 'O' levels leading naturally to a first-class degree in Computer Science, is an extremely successful Project Manager in the USA, while my sister holds an MBA and is making a successful career in the fields of health and services.

In Africa, your predecessors, your heritage, are important. As who we are now, my siblings and I, as the adults we have become, we still offer our father our due respect and continue to want to make him proud.

From Hood to Headship

From a young age, I had been made aware that I am the descendant of the Fante King – Fante, a tribe of Ghana, West Africa. I am also the daughter of the Ga rulers of the capital city, Accra. I am from a mixed tribe, both with extremely strong pride in their heritage and esteemed by their respective people. There was no room for mediocrity in our family. We worked hard, achieved highly, and demonstrated class. Woe betide anyone who fancied themselves a freeloader or didn't understand the merit with which we held our heads up high, and who showed the world the opposite, being lazy, not hard-working or of credibility. Dare anyone to bring shame to the families.

I was the product of strong and established women.

My paternal grandmother was the local seamstress and designer of outfits for the rich and famous. She was married to my grandfather, an esteemed member of the council, well-educated and respected, with children of equally high standing, including an archbishop. (My dad almost went down that route.) It might interest you to know that she was also a royalist and loved the Queen.

My maternal grandmother was the only female in Accra in her time who owned multiple businesses across the city and, it has been said, took no prisoners. A respectable feat to behold at a time when women were still mocked if they chose careers, let alone pathways which seemed 'unwomanly' and far from being the stay-at-home mothers raising children. Did I mention she physically gave birth to 13 children too? This included two sets of twins.

So, in terms of tenacity and strength, I would like to think that some of that may have trickled down to me, hopefully.

Somehow, from over the seas, middle-class expectations and aspirations wove their way into our family. We were not allowed to forget where we originated from, ever.

It is recognised that the reasons for arriving in the UK for the African and Caribbean communities differed. Unfortunately, the residue of the diaspora has led to some of us, in particular the older generations, not understanding this and losing a little love for our fellow humans.

Dad was in my earlier days of life probably part of that guard, not understanding the plight of the Caribbean. This wasn't helped by the visible sight of what he termed the 'layabouts' on the estate who seemed to roam around aimlessly, ambitionless and without seeking to give back to society – no job, no prospects, victims of the state.

Being a first-generation Black African in the UK, there were many demons I had to challenge but what I always sensed was a mission to bring my people – be they Black African or Black Caribbean – together as one. I would often find myself defending the perception of my Caribbean friends in debates with my dad.

As intelligent as he was, the legacy of divide and conquer, the residue of what had created the resentment from the history that the Africans had 'sold out' their brothers and sisters who ended up in the Caribbean, or that the Caribbeans were not strong enough to fight and yielded, ran too deep into the wounds. It is all nonsense, of course, but British history teaching with its missing truths has a lot to answer for.

As a child, I remember hanging onto my identity and dignity. Many would often deny my heritage when I told them I was Black African and this I used to my advantage, as you could not easily determine which part of the diaspora I originated from. Blending into the Caribbean scene for me came easily.

However, it did not sit comfortably with me when I often heard statements like: *'You? You're not African. You don't look African.'*

As a child, I didn't yet have the vernacular or even confidence to respond. What would I say? As I grew up, my retorts would simply be things like: '*What does an African look like?*'

My questioners would often have a look of confusion or bemusement, having been made to pause and think. It even affected relationships. I recall a young man exclaiming loudly on the phone: '*No way – you're not an Af!*'

How dare he? Let's just say that he didn't have the gall to call me again after I dealt with him. I had refined the art of educating and shaming someone who failed to recognise that 'Black' was really what we were, together, and that imperialism was not right amongst our own.

Where I lived, you would hear conversations in English, some English being peppered with European accents, Portuguese, French, Eastern (though much later on) but mostly either UK-Black London accents or 'Jamaicanesque' twang. Of course, authentic accents were also to be heard, likely from the highly influential Jamaican culture existing there – from grannies with their shopping trolleys clogging up the aisles on Harlesden's busy pavements or from the mouth of the recent arrival.

And in the heart of Harlesden, amongst the several betting shops better known as 'bookies', barbershops, off-licences, chicken shops, nail bars and utility shops, stood Harlesden library.

I used to visit Harlesden library a lot as a child. The oasis of calm in the centre of the bustling high street. From there I took out the Linguaphone cassette and book sets on loan. I experimented with French, Spanish, German and Italian. I was fascinated when I discovered these. I would pop one cassette into my player and read along. Opening my mouth to say aloud what I read was automatic. I was instantly propelled, out of Harlesden and Church Road, into my imaginary country abroad.

From Hood to Headship

Though I didn't know it, I was clocking up the 10,000 hours of practice to be an expert, according to Matthew Syed (Syed, 2010). I didn't fancy German too much; somehow the language felt cold and mechanical. I eventually retired from Italian, even though I enjoyed its melodic-sounding linguistics. I became hooked on French and Spanish.

I loved the sophisticated sounds of French and the open, jolly intonation and diction of Spanish. It was my early form of 'me time' when it was just me immersed in my Linguaphone sets. I renewed them over and over again, so much that eventually I just kept hold of them. I'm sure the library wrote to me to return them but who reads letters at the age of 10? Sorry, Harlesden library. Thankfully, we have moved on from cassettes now, so these are definitely not missed.

No matter where I lived as I grew up, I always ended up returning to Harlesden. If I wanted my 'hard food', a term used by Jamaicans to refer to the likes of yam plantain, sweet potato and pumpkin, and I also wanted the Jamaican staple, ackee, which I loved, there was one well-known cash and carry in Harlesden that everybody went to. So I did too.

A walk down Park Parade would have me observing the fluorescent colours of shiny leggings or outlandish and exposing clothing, or simultaneously walking past the barbershop overhearing conversations as the men shouted out at the ladies. As I grew up to be one of those ladies walking by, I learned how to 'fix my face', as we would say. It was a way of putting on the mask or expression that said: 'Don't bother messing with me today. I am not in the mood and I will truly cuss you out!'

Most young men knew how to read the expression but also avoided the risk of being publicly humiliated by such a lady, so it often had the desired effect. They would leave me alone, or better still, use more gentle greeting phrases.

I began to realise that this 'expression' I had when I fixed my face would stand me in good stead when I had to use facial expressions in the classroom.

Mastering 'the look' came in handy later on in a multitude of encounters, as a very young teacher, as a mother, and even later, at the big round table of senior leaders.

Then there would be honking of horns as a driver discovered he was blocked in by relentless and inconsiderate double parking, or someone did a U-turn in the middle of the busy traffic to squeeze into the spot across the road – it was always entertaining.

Sadly, the entertainment has not always been positive and Harlesden is synonymous with youths killed with knives and days of shootings. Having links with the area, my heart jumps every time I hear of such incidents, hoping it will not be news of someone I know. In the Black community, it can feel as though you are less than six degrees separated all the time.

The community is large, well-linked, and deeply true to the sense of community, so the possibility is always there. Unlike your average middle-class English citizen, you never rest easy when the BBC begins with the words, 'A man has been shot ...'; that's just the way it is. It's a tragedy that, in the UK, the people surrounded by this just have to carry on, knowing that there will not be enough done to eradicate the violence and the perpetual disadvantages.

Teachers in schools with children from these areas must know and, if not, learn about these circumstances that their students navigate daily to best serve them. The struggle is real and probably unbelievable to some who have never heard of the areas or cannot believe that in such a 'westernised and civilised' country as this, such crime and danger exists. It's a whole different world for some people.

I lived for 22 years in Church End Estate, a 5-minute walk away, but was always in Harlesden. I saw the changing face of my estate as I grew up. I navigated through life sometimes succumbing to the ills of estate culture, such as the time an ex-boyfriend drove me to a 'drugs sell' without my knowledge, and other times I had the intuition or sheer bloody-mindedness to say 'no' or avoid getting involved or being associated with events which had lasting impacts on the lives of others.

Surrounding ourselves with like-minded friends is such an important part of growing up – it can literally save your life. So can the power of parental discipline and power – single-handedly or not.

As others who were less familiar with the area moved into it as part of the regeneration, the cohesion of the community began to disintegrate. I had become the 'community mother' to the younger ones growing up. The group of young men who gathered at the bottom of the staircase showed me respect as I did to them. There was a shared understanding but, as newer faces moved in, the community spirit moved out.

The area became more and more hostile, particularly among some of the younger ones. Riddled with gun crime, knife crime and the sounds of police sirens, it would no longer be my choice of location to raise my family.

I loved Harlesden. I felt Harlesden. I ate, slept and danced Harlesden. I lived Harlesden.

I am Black African.

I lose count of how many times I have reflected and thought about how my background has helped me in my career.

Being of West African descent, amalgamating the nuances of Black Caribbean and Black British culture, not living too far away from my students, meant it was rare for the sort of children I was dealing with to accuse me of never understanding them. You might argue that, had I started teaching in a leafy part of the world with the wealthy, middle-class, all English-speaking, and highly aspirational attitudes, I might not have experienced quite the same sensation, or that I had what it took to succeed in this arena. I would argue the converse.

I may have had a working-class lifestyle but I was surrounded by a global family who had middle-class expectations.

My 'middle-class' West African heritage and strong faith background, coupled with the absolute sheer impossibility to consider anything less than a further education qualification that imbued my entire family of doctors, lawyers, independent businessmen and women, an archbishop, and of course teachers, probably makes a good argument for why I could not turn out any other way. I was raised with middle-class expectations, and I was, in all ways, except in location.

These ingredients sprinkled into the 'Super Woman' I always aspire to be. Everyone is a distinct dish made up of different ingredients and together we fill this world with a recipe book of battle broths, resilience risottos, and success-story soups, washed down with fine appreciation wine.

From Hood to Headship

(Ratcliff, J iCanvas, https://www.icanvas.com/canvas-print/super-shadows-kid-of-steel-jrf71#1PC6-40x26)

This is a picture that was gifted to me when I got the headship. It helps me remember the journey I have made from the little girl from northwest London. I believe it is a copy of the 'Super Shadows Kid of Steel' by **Jason Ratliff** canvas art print.

What hurts only makes you stronger

2. Mother's Day

'Our individual identities are dependent on our parenting, and our life experiences and how both have shaped our sense of self.' (Viv Grant, 2014)

It smelled horrible. The perfume that the woman wore who was adamant she stood next to me and cried her loudest cries. Who was she? Perhaps she needed to make everyone know who she was. Perhaps she was truly a good friend of the family, but I didn't know her. She wore the colour purple. A richly deep, velvety purple that somehow matched the horrid smell of her perfume. I will never forget that scent, ever. My stomach churned, my eyes were so swollen from crying and I just wanted to scream. That wasn't my mother in there. No way – in a coffin? She looked so different. Her face had darkened, she looked lean, unsmiling. I was only used to seeing my mother smiling, and yet with her very stony, melancholy expression, she was surrounded by all these people. A very strange thought in my head was: 'If she loves me, then why is she leaving me? Perhaps she will come back and get me, or does she want me to jump into the coffin with her? Maybe that's what I am supposed to do.'

I felt myself urged forward, my feet dragged slowly nearer to her, even though I knew I didn't want to, I tried to resist. I couldn't. As I got closer, a hand grabbed the back of my furry hood and dragged me back, my arms flailing – now I was wailing. This could not be really happening. 'Was it really happening?'

I wanted to die, I felt like I was dying; inside I was. Thankfully, there is a saying: 'What doesn't kill you makes you stronger.' I had a vivid imagination as a child. So vivid it would cause me fright sometimes to go upstairs alone or be in the dark. Today, that imagination created my darkest time. Aged 6, I was experiencing something no human at that age ought to feel. The death of my mother, and its aftermath. The gut-wrenching, ultimate anguish and internal pain that was felt from that day forward is nothing I have ever felt again. My dad said that it was because I was so hurt. I always remember dad saying this to me, like a mantra. He said having experienced death as a child, nothing more could hurt me. Meaning, he understood how badly this hurt. Yes, I would feel pain from other things, but this had probably been the worst it would ever get. He always told me that I would not allow anything to make me feel this way again and that I was protected. 'Be bold,' he would say, 'and always go for what you want. Speak up! Speak clearly! Don't mutter. Come on, Miriam, be bold.'

Mum had lost her battle to breast cancer in 1979. Her desire was that we would move out of the concrete jungle, which was the ninth floor of Prothero House on the Stonebridge estate. She wanted so badly for us to move into the new maisonette being built on Church Road, about a 10-minute walk away on the other side of Harlesden. Sadly, she didn't make it. She passed before she had the chance to even see the new home. I remember so clearly us talking about how we would decorate the home. She was mean at crochet and also used to create the rugs with the Readicut latch-hook system which I always created with her.

Experiences carve us out, shape who we become, and this adverse traumatic experience did that to me. In a way, I put my inner strength and tenacity down to having contended with grief at such an early age. Only time healed me and time it took. For about 30 years I could not talk or even think about it without a tear in sight. When I tell others that I lost my mother at the age of 6, I feel their empathy, not just see it. What I also know is that they recognise the trauma and, without verbalising it, know that such events can have adverse effects.

They call them ACEs – Adverse Childhood Experiences – within three key areas: neglect, abuse, household dysfunction. There is a very good report on this in *Adverse Childhood Experiences in London* (Bullock, 2019). It states:

> more recently, the conversation has broadened, with increasing recognition that other childhood experiences can prove impactful on the stress response, including those that are felt at community, rather than household, level. Racism, discrimination, bullying, community violence and poverty are being acknowledged as comparable, if not greater sources of adversity and as risk factors for toxic stress.

Any child suffering four or more ACEs is likely to experience a direct consequence on their health and/or wellbeing. Although my mother's bereavement does not fit neatly into the original categories, you can see in the diagram below that bereavement features in the updated tree diagram taken from the study.

The impact of ACEs, traumatic events that occur in childhood (0–17 years), can be evident several years into adulthood and in some cases never abate. The chances of ACEs increase dramatically, and are therefore more prevalent, in communities riddled with low income, crime and deprivation.

They in turn impact negatively on education, job opportunities and income-earning potential as well as health and wellbeing. Studies to recognise and improve the life chances for those more susceptible are now well-documented and this knowledge features in some of the Professional Development (PD) in schools. But schools cannot fix communities on their own. Just saying.

Figure 2: Adverse Childhood Experiences and Adverse Community Environments – Updating the adversity tree

Adverse Childhood Experiences

Domestic violence

Emotional abuse

Physical or emotional neglect

Alcohol misuse

Violence or coercion

Bereavement

Sexual abuse

Mental illness in the household

Drug misuse

Inhumane treatment, e.g. experiencing or witnessing torture

Poor maternal mental health

Incarceration

Adult responsibilities e.g. caring

Parental separation or conflict

Community disruption

Violence in the community

Discrimination or prejudice

Poverty

Poor housing quality and affordability

Lack of opportunity or economic mobility

Housing insecurity or homelessness

Adverse Community Environments

Source: Author, adapted from Ellis and Deitz and Young Minds

Image taken from M. Bullock (2019), *Adverse Child Experiences in London*, p. 17

My trauma has never gone away. Being resilient is one of those things you cannot be taught. You can only ever be moulded into a resilient person, by going through some of the rough. It's like emerging like a diamond, hard as a rock but beautiful as ever. Maybe not always beautiful, but resilience is certainly a characteristic to be admired.

So, when each year Mother's Day came around, my resilience was put to the test.

Mother's Day 1: 'Happy Mother's Da… ,' she began to say to me, until she saw the sadness in my eyes. 'Oh, I'm really sorry.'

Thankfully, I had an emotionally intelligent 'sista-friend' from childhood, Myline. She loved me like a sister. We refer to each other as 'sisters from another mother'. There wasn't a day that went by without meeting up with my sista-friend, as I like to call her. Every year, I had to endure the same 'Happy Mother's Day' announcements with friends, mainly at school. Often, many were either unaware of how this statement would impact me, or unlike my sista-friend, lacked the emotional intelligence to see the awkward smile I held in my face, a sort of smiling whilst gritting through the 'ouch' of the term. My response was always in my head, and it always said, 'I have not got a mother. My mother is dead, so it's not a happy Mother's Day for me at all.'

Over the years, the pain of this statement waned. It sort of melted away with the years, many years. I believe, though, that going through the gritted teeth, smiling days, feeling the churn, and deciding over time how I would celebrate my mother, even though she was no longer with me, became character-building. Eventually, I taught myself to honour my mother on Mother's Day. I had one burning thought which was wondering how I would feel if blessed with children of my own. Later in my life, I was indeed blessed with them. More about them later.

Often, I think about the fact that she is looking down on me from the sky, feeling very proud of my accomplishments. I am gutted not to be able to speak to her in person and talk to her about my highs and lows. Still, I know that even in all the anguish of her passing, and the feelings of inadequacy that I feel it led me to have, my becoming the strong Black female I am is in some part due to the struggle that has been with me over the years, to overcome the loss of a guiding star, a mother, the one everyone calls out to when they are in need.

'"Mother", the person we grumble to the most and who treats us the best.' I remember reading that on a plaque brought from the seaside resort of Margate at a friend's house. When the going gets tough, everyone wants their mum.

As a teacher and leader, and definitely as a wife and mother, sometimes I want to say 'I want my mum', but I don't even utter the words out loud as I know it is an impossible request. It feels unfair to even think like this but grown women do still need their mums; to grumble, to cry, to gossip and to laugh with.

In my role as a headteacher, I have on occasion felt the same need to cry out to someone and they are not there. Usually, because there isn't quite the right person to turn to or I choose not to share my questioning with another for fear of showing my lack of knowledge or indication that I was not 'ready'. What happens next is I might pray, but usually, the answer does come from within; I find a way. Maybe this has been preparation for this. Never underestimate the power of your experiences in shaping you.

Dad raised us and he did a bloody good job. It was never easy. Protecting us from the draw of the stereotypical mishaps of estate culture was his second job. He made plenty of sacrifices including giving up the opportunity to go fully and deeply into accountancy as he should have done. He never ever settled for mediocrity in his work and worked extremely hard at everything he did. As I learned about this as I got older, I felt a sense of guilt.

Perhaps if I had not come along a bit later, life might have been a bit easier for him. I am sure he felt a sense of disappointment, especially after having attended Oxford University as part of his journey toward his career. This disappointment could have easily transferred to my siblings and me. If these disappointments and professional failings of my father took root, they could have easily shaped my feelings of hope and shaped my vision of who I could become.

In some ways, I have been spending my life trying to undo this pain. This is where I say things to myself like 'Well, without a mum, I have not really learned the best way to mother' or cook, or other seemingly assumed motherly traits. I know that this thought pattern has served to make me look for recognition and success to undo some of this.

Seeking recognition. It can be good and it can be bad at times, but no one is immune to the cortisol that rises up within oneself when being recognised for the contributions one makes to society; it does help to encourage. I have learnt that recognition is one of my values. The downside is it can lead to seeking approval, and an insatiable appetite for recognition and success which does not always come from where you expect it to.

As a leader in education today, I try to 'live and not laminate' my values. I do my best to ensure I value and recognise the worth of those I lead, using whatever systems I can, knowing that individuals bring with them their own experiences or even ACEs and for the most part start off doing the best they can. It is also a critical element of recruiting and retaining staff. I aim to be a good leader because I attempt to reflect this value in my daily walk. As Brené Brown says, 'Leaders lead from the heart, not from hurt' (Brown, 2018).

(Me, right side of mum, age 6 and my family,)

3. The Computer Analyst

'Teeth Do Not See Poverty.'
(Masai proverb)

'Give me back my headphones!' my brother John shouted. Meanwhile, I was doubled up in fits of laughter on the worn-out carpet on the stairs of our two-floored, inner-city estate maisonette. The carpet was so worn, you could see, and feel, the wooden steps underneath quite clearly. We couldn't afford to have any redecoration, so the maisonette was allowed to just fade and wear over the years. Some days, funds were so low that my brother, sister and I would share items made for one individual, and I am talking about food.

I remember one Saturday morning, just the three of us at home and my sister had woken up early, found the only egg in the fridge, and cooked herself up a lovely breakfast with the last egg, the last two slices of bread, a tin of beans and a cup of tea using her favourite, tinned milk. We used tinned milk for everything. Clearly it had more lasting power than the fresh sort, which I only tasted if I stayed at a friend's house, the friend whose mother had taken me in as her own child since meeting my dad in a distressed state, running late to collect me from school one day.

Tinned milk was our substitute for our cornflakes – not Kellogg's – mixed with water, and voilà! You had 'fresh milk'. Sad times. We always found something to smile or even laugh about. 'Teeth do not see poverty.'

As my brother and I smelt the food, we rushed downstairs to see her walking quickly to the living room (she stayed there) to eat all alone. She was laughing at us as she knew she had made it and had said she was starving so she couldn't wait for us to wake up.

Just as she was sitting down on the sofa, her hand wobbled, losing balance of her tray and over toppled her plate with the single egg, bread and beans. Our mouths were ajar in shock and John and I burst out laughing in absolute hysterics.

'Shame! Shame!' we kept saying.

Sis wasn't laughing. She looked as though she was about to cry. Somehow, the tea remained on the tray. We can laugh about it now.

Back to my moment with John though. John was fuming, his eyes were red and he was clenching his fists. I knew that he would never strike me and I carried on being the annoying little sister. I had been tormenting him all morning as I had no other business to tend to. He, on the other hand, had his examinations to prepare for. That would make me 12 years old and him 16.

At that moment, little did I know that I was going to eat a major serving of humble pie, as this round-headed, want-to-be muscly brother of mine, who buried his head in music, would go on to become a mini-genius, achieving a string of grade As in his 'O' levels and securing his place at University College London to study Computer Science. If it were now, let's just say the grade 9 would need a 9+ for his level of academic excellence. A feat I could only imagine when I got to my time in the last year of secondary school. He did, in fact, end up working with computers and extremely successfully doing so.

My big brother John, Johnny B as he is known to family and friends, was in love with his white and red headphones set. The cassette tapes would be played over and over again and it was really exciting as it had auto-reverse so it didn't need to stop but just continued playing. On this rainy spring day, I had decided not to go out to play but had filled my time hiding some of his treasures and dared to separate him from his beloved headphones. I had achieved something dad had not been able to do, despite his strictness.

John went into his room and slammed the door. I knew then that I had really pissed him off. We got on so well, usually listening to 'tunes', old school soul, jazz funk, electro-funk, the sounds of Africa Bambaata and Soulsonic Force and other early rap songs, bopping our heads and having friendly challenges about who knew the best tracks. I had spoiled this. What was I going to do now? The fun had stopped and he was in his room, without his headphones. Bad move. Eventually, I took the missing beloved instrument from its hiding place and humbly knocked on his door to go in. I think he was so relieved to have them back, he just let me in and tenderly took them from me, placing them on his small bookshelf.

'What are you doing?' I asked. 'I'm studying, I've got an exam on Friday,' he replied. It was only Sunday. Dad had not been easy on John, perhaps being the only boy child or just the fear of him being swallowed up by the estate kids. Dad ensured that he studied. I saw this, and I knew it must be good for him and, therefore, good for me.

The studying culture passed on from one sibling to the next. I admired his ability to just focus, spend dedicated time with his books and learn. Even when we had spent hours on the estate roller skating, using the roads as our playground to travel by personal wheels, staying out so late that dad would need to come and embarrassingly find us, he would still return and study. His destination: computer analyst. I didn't even know what that was but I knew the computer was the way to go.

When our best family-friends bought a Commodore 64 (C64) computer, we were instinctively drawn to it. Its power of persuasion, that whispered 'play with me', was so strong. Children up and down the country were hooked on this with games such as Pacman and Space Invaders. There was something magical and addictive even then about these first-phase computers and about clicking to make things happen. It is no surprise we have the war on technology with children now.

When it was my turn at school to talk about what I wanted to be as an adult, it seemed to roll off the tongue. 'A computer analyst,' I said confidently, looking at the faces to see their expressions, hoping I had impressed someone, or at least bamboozled them. It seems the only person I impressed was Ms Simmonds, our middle-aged, loud and eccentric primary school class teacher who took no nonsense. Her eyes bulged as I said this. Unlike some of my peers, who unfortunately had to contend with the labels of being 'educationally subnormal', being treated as in some sort of academic need, rendering their thoughts and ambitions as incomprehensible and unachievable, Ms Simmonds did not put me down. She did not express any glaringly low expectations, ridden with covertly racist comments, such as asking me, 'Are you sure? Don't you want to be a nurse, or a shop assistant?' or any of those types of sentences that I know many have been used to hearing.

Perhaps I was lucky. All of us in her class were lucky. I would say Ms Simmonds was one of my early champions. Ms Simmonds simply duly noted the phrase 'computer analyst' on the board and then in her book and said, 'That is very interesting. How did you know about this job?'

'My brother wants to do this and I think I want to do this too,' I said.

'Well, I am glad you have thought about what you want to do in the future. It sounds like a very interesting job,' she continued, and went to the next student.

There was no tone of surprise in her voice, no lack of belief, no questioning interrogatively about my clear lack of actual real understanding of the role. A bible verse in Proverbs talks about the power of the tongue. It reads: 'Death and life are in the power of the tongue, and those who love it will eat its fruit' (Proverbs 18:21).

With our words, we can edify, build up, encourage and uplift or we can pull down, crush and destroy, depending on the words we choose to say. The best teachers know this and know the power of their tongue, in and outside of classrooms.

What Ms Simmonds had done, unwittingly, from her choice of words, was make it seem realistic to me. She had made me feel as though it was a possible destination, that there were no other considerations to be made about why it might be challenging for me to get there or why I had thought about this and then proposed another, perhaps less technical, position.

Ms Simmonds clearly knew my background – everyone did, because my dad was the one regularly arriving late to collect me after school. The story of how he had become a single parent was known by everyone, as it seemed so tragic at the time. I was a child from one of the affordable accommodations on the local estate surrounding this primary school, so it was clear that we were not from the houses nearby, probably mortgaged by families who were earning salaries that trebled my dad's.

Brené Brown talks about 'people in the stands' of the arena. She talks of the 'box seats' which are filled with those who have built the arena to benefit people who look like them but to look down upon those who differ from them. Those who differ in terms of race, class, sexual orientation, ability and status. These people seem to make it clear that these differences exist by their act of continuous comparisons between individuals or groups. They look at you and have 'already determined your odds, based on stereotypes, misinformation and fear', she says (Brown, 2018). These people come from a position of 'privilege'. I am sure we can all think of individuals who fit this description and feed into our feelings of self-worth and/or shame. Ms Simmonds did not do this.

There was one thing we had in common though and that was coming to a school of faith. Perhaps this was our luck. Our school was a Church of England school and every Wednesday we had to attend the local church for service in the morning. I can't help but feel as though there are some principles in faith schools supported by the families that attend them, most of whom are of the faith, which support a sort of principled ethos, one that encourages ambition and kindness and eliminates bias. Perhaps, by virtue of the teachings in the Christian faith, this was the result. Ms Simmonds' response, as minor as it may seem, has stayed with me and contributes to my thought process today, whenever interacting with the thousands of young people I have come into contact with.

I believe that a conversation about the future aspirations of children can never be taken lightly. Elements of conversations linger in the minds of children, they feed the imagination and allow them to think of what they can become. They make the unimaginable tangible, reachable and experiential.

There is a catalogue of events that allow a child to consider how far in life they may be able to go and what is within their reach. In our household, we played hard but we also studied hard. We saw each other studying hard and it was normal. It was just what you did. School for us was never going to end at 16 but at 21, after you had finished university, and that was just the way it was for our family, immediate and extended. Plus I hated the look of our flat in need of redecoration three times over and I wanted to become an adult that could do something about it.

It was usual to have books lying around, exercise books, encyclopaedias, comics, magazines, and even catalogues.

Studying was just something to do. We did it because we wanted to get good grades. We did it because it had been drummed into our heads by our father and family that were not even in the UK but still resided in Ghana. We did it because we knew it was important currency, and it would pay to get a good education and therefore a good job. We did it because, one day, we knew that a good job would allow us to fully carpet the staircase in our home.

Your USP is the substance of your authentic self

4. School Days – Class of '88

Wouldn't you agree that a school expeirnce is probably one of the most universal experiences around the world? Even in the most remote places, most people have had some experience of going to some sort of school. It would be remiss of me not to acknowledge that it is still considered a privilege in some parts of the world where attending school is still out of reach. Even the desire to be at school means everyone knows what the institution of schooling is, or should be. I can honestly say that my school days were some of the best days of my life.

It was at school I learned an extra-curricular syllabus called 'building friendships' which included my explosion into puberty and with it the butterflies, stomach churns, fears and uncertainties of romance. It contributes to how I understand being a young person in every class I take, and why peer pressure is so strong.

Being raised in North Weezy, learning my 'don't mess with me' face and enduring a bit of rough on the estate must have made me quite formidable. I was not a bully nor bullied but was very close to individuals who were and attempted in my own way to prevent them being victim to it. I always thought it interesting that I was not subjected to it, even though I was with those who were. I felt strongly about how they were treated and still feel very passionately, even to the point of emotion, today.

It is not tolerated at all wherever I work, but when I had a taste of it as an adult, it was a challenge to overcome.

My friend Irvin and I had a love for and a shared taste in music. I remember the days when I sat in what were the Craft, Design and Technology lessons, and snuck one earpiece into my ear when my buddy Irvin would sneak into his ear the other. We would bop our heads along to the sounds of some rare grooves, reggae, hip hop, swing beat, soul, or whatever sounds he introduced me to and sounds I would eventually end up raving, far too much, to as a young adult.

In school was where I discovered my roots and built the foundation of my friendships which continue to this day, and included one of my now late best friends, Cody, otherwise known as the great 'Tittla'. Spending hours on end on the telephone line came naturally to us as we spoke of our dreams and ambitions, of what we would become as adults. Cody was so funny too and I spent most of my lessons in Statistics sitting next to him, holding my bladder, as I would not be allowed to go to the toilet for fear of causing disruption to the class.

It made me focus to get the work done though, so I could finally release all the laughing juice out of my body.

I was no saint, but I was not a little devil either. Well, not until the Religious Studies teacher told me I was going to fail everything. My style of 'feisty' came out when required, let's just say. There is nothing quite so satisfying and that makes you driven than proving someone wrong, which I did in my final year.

I remember Cody teasing my friend Amy and me as we, according to him, sailed through the Statistics exams with ease, whilst he struggled along. He expressed this to us on leaving the exam hall. He used to say that we were 'ginnals' (a Jamaican term for someone who tricks you) because while we giggled and laughed as he provided jokes galore, we studied, while he was failing. What we didn't do was 'bring him along' which is a phrase I often use when teaching and students have friends not performing quite where they should be: 'Bring your friend along.'

My school in the inner-city London borough of Westminster also taught me the importance that diversity, multiculturalism and background have on your success. We mingled with children from the local estates as well as those who were children of ambassadors to important countries. School made us who we are today. Sadly, a stabbing that occurred some years later at a neighbouring school also highlighted to us that we were no different, or excluded from the chilling realities of gang crime, because we were in Westminster, at the heart of inner-city life.

Side by side, my diverse friends and I had shared circumstances, shared values, and being a Church of England school, these were shared Christian values. I often wonder, perhaps this is what made us what and who we are. Maybe?

Many of us went on to be successful individuals in our own ways and remain friends to this day. After the establishment of WhatsApp, there were about 30 of us who communicated daily on WhatsApp well into our mid-40s.

It was a great keeping-in-touch tool, but the transition to headship meant something had to give in terms of my time.

We all know how addictive social media can be and preparing for headship won my time, sealing my decision to leave this social media group, although I remain in contact with individuals.

All my experiences at school taught me to be tough, feisty, have difficult conversations, to question and challenge. Little did I know too, that when my RE teacher said I would amount to nothing, this determination to prove someone wrong would lead to the day I went back and showed him my B grade. In Year 10, I began the course of English Literature but, after the first A- I received, I left.

Yes, I dropped English Literature, preferring not to spend my Friday period 5s falling asleep beside the radiator in the cold autumn term. That's when I transferred to Statistics.

My teacher wouldn't speak to me. Becoming a teacher allowed me, however, to gather snippets of the English Literature I missed, so at times you might find me slipping into the Year 10 *A Christmas Carol* lesson or the Year 11 *An Inspector Calls* and even stealing a read of my son's GCSE *Macbeth* revision guide. As the saying goes, it's never too late – a message that is important to pass on to students all the time.

Looking back at my disadvantaged status, I believe dad did damn well. I did not miss out on a single trip, despite the disadvantage. It has to be said that in those days grants did exist, although there were still never enough funds; however, that did not deter dad from finding and making up the difference.

What I describe here is contrary to the experiences and outcomes of several others raised in similar contexts. Unlike those who had to experience the hugely and infamous 'educationally subnormal' misnomers of being tossed into the relentless cycle of remedial classes for those apparently less educated. This was not a term used in my era, or in my school. Schooling for some Black children seemed like a lottery.

I happened to be fortunate in my choices and in my freedom to choose where I wanted to be educated. My primary school sat in the heart of Church End Estate, but it was a church school. Whilst the automatic and natural pathway for most receiving schooling in the vicinity was to attend the local schools, I had refused to put any of these schools on my application form.

The absence of my dad several evenings of the week, leaving us to tend to our own business, made us grow up very prematurely and there I was too, deciding my fate by selecting my future high school education.

I had decided that I wanted to go outside of Brent and, like a few in my class, wanted to go to one of the secondary church schools, either St Mary's or St Augustine's. One in the borough of Barnet, the other in Westminster.

What were my chances of getting in? Pretty good, and I ended up at St Augustine's – the inner-city church school with a totally eclectic mix of children from different corners of the earth by their heritage. Children of ambassadors who lived further north, towards Edgware Road, of Arabic heritage with very wealthy parents, to those in the west who were bus travellers, generations of Caribbeans who had outlived the Windrush and were survivors of the riots in Notting Hill, a stone's throw away.

My small primary school peer group came from the south of Brent.

A church school that went to mass every Wednesday, observed Christian principles and had an underlying culture based on the common desires of most of the parents, to do even better than they had done. There was something special about St Augustine's. It didn't stop us from having fights under the flats in the car park, or bunking and running off to Granville to play pool, only to scatter and race back when the head and her team descended upon the centre; our lookout had failed, too busy eating the take-away he had managed to buy and thereby leaving us victim to our school police.

I remember that day, I was so scared of what my dad would do when he found out. We all were. We were actually bothered that our parents could do something about this.

A little different to some of the young people nowadays.

All of these school days' experiences certainly drove me to become the individual I am today, at least playing a major part in my make-up and now also helping me to understand why I am the teacher I have become.

From Hood to Headship

Being a teacher of French was never my ambition to begin with, but I owe it all to Madame Nouqueret. What I would not give to see her in person and say, 'Thank you, I am your protégé indeed, the one you wrote "Francophile" to in her leaver's book!' The little Black disadvantaged English-speaking chic from the ends, who became a teacher of modern foreign languages, opening up the world through communication to thousands of children along the way.

5. Disadvantaged Uni-girl

'If you want to go fast, go alone.
If you want to go far, go together.'
(African proverb)

I'm not an Oxbridge graduate. I'm not even a graduate from a Russell Group or high-tariff university. I still hold a degree and still hold a postgraduate degree qualification. In education, in some ways, it doesn't matter. This is because you are there to enable others to do even better than you. The starting blocks are not in the same position for everyone.

My university was in London. Big mistake. I was saved because of the course I had chosen to pursue. Studying modern languages, you would be hard-pushed back then to encounter someone who was Black and even more hard-pressed to meet another who originated from London. This meant less distraction for me, but loneliness in shared experiences. Studying languages has always had this connotation of being for the 'elite' members of society. I saw a flavour of this among my counterparts.

Some had holidayed every summer since birth in Nice or even on the coasts of Monaco. There were the young individuals who had fallen into studying languages because they were the offspring of ambassadors of their host countries, studying French and Spanish who came from places like France and Spain, naturally, but also Ivory Coast, Colombia and Mexico. Then there was me, living in a council maisonette in Church End Estate, travelling daily on the tube to attend lectures. I had chosen to stay in London as I couldn't bring myself to leave dad alone at home. My small contribution from a part-time job meant he didn't have to continue to find a way for me as he still laboured at his Highgate-based job.

To me, the fact that I worked as I studied revealed the greatest difference in my university study experience to others in my cohort. I held a part-time job, while I remember some of my peers lived in residences – not halls – paid for by their parents and had untapped income they received from their parents in the form of a salary. Thank God for the UK grant scheme, as otherwise university for me would have been a non-starter. I know this is not unique for me but, coupled with what I am about to tell you, it made for an insightful experience of being a Black female Londoner at university on a language course.

One of the peers in my group was clearly not used to studying in London; having done the reverse of moving out of London, he had moved in. He was overcome by my blackness and made little effort to hide it. He would try to touch my hair. He asked intrusive questions and his comments were embarrassingly naïve. From his very upper-middle background, I could sense that he had also led a very sheltered life. It was fascinating for me living in London. Fortunately, this course also brought together people from a wide range of ethnic backgrounds and it got so bad, I didn't even need to be the one to tell him to back off. I had not yet encountered people who saw Black people as a phenomenon.

Well, that was until I did the very thing that drew me to the course in the first place – I spent a year abroad. I was drawn to do this course at this university precisely because I would spend a year abroad. I knew it would broaden my horizons and I believe this is an experience every child should have – travel.

My time in Paris, France, was awesome. However, before that, I had spent seven months in Alicante, in Spain, where I would walk the streets and be heckled at with 'hola morena, rubia'. 'Morena' means black girl and 'rubia' means blonde. I was not alone. It seemed in this part of the world they had seen neither black people nor blondes in the flesh! We lived right in the centre of town and, by the end of the time staying there, the entire community knew who we were.

Many can access this now, but there exists a great chasm separating the haves and the have-nots. Some go on to university as it is just a natural progression for them, like generations before them; meanwhile, those disadvantaged children who study hard get to a point where they realise that their dreams to go further and be more come to a dispiriting halt, due to finances. To put it bluntly, it just isn't fair.

I remember my uni days. I remember that, when it got to year 2, I almost gave in as I found it too difficult to balance my home, work, and study life. I was also on the edge – partying too much, having too much fun with friends outside of uni. I began arriving late and not really paying too much attention. I submitted sub-standard essays as I lost the motivation to put my all into what I was studying. I guess, inside, I feared I would not make it. Not being joined in a shared university experience by many others from the 'hood', I didn't feel able to share what I was going through. Aside from my brother, there was really only one other, a friend who lived near me but didn't study with me. At least I could discuss the thoughts in my head around the demands of university study.

I remember a special French friend who sat me down, told me about my wayward tendencies and, being the leader she was, orchestrated that my 'tutor group' rallied behind me to finish that all-important essay to get to the next term. She shifted my paradigm. She made me examine what I wanted for myself. It wasn't a race. She wasn't competing against me. Heck, I would have lost anyway. She helped me move on with the support and encouragement of others. She was not Black. She was not even from London, demonstrating that our allies can come from whoever has a genuine volition to help another and stand beside you.

I only hope there can be more like her to look out for others from the 'hood' who reach that point and need someone to help them go on – to go farther.

If I can change the paradigm of even just one child, help them see there is a wider world, that there are others both like them and unlike them that they can learn from, give them the chance to experience higher education, then I will have done what I set out to do.

Every leader has something that motivates and drives them. There is usually a goal to work towards and a purpose to fill. This is one of mine. The beauty of being a leader in education is that the impact of fulfilling that purpose in others can last a lifetime.

I fell into teaching. That moment of anti-climax after our uni talk will stay with me. It was a broad course of study so I had applied to do journalism where all the subjects I studied might come into play. Our lecturer put the idea of teaching in my head. So I checked it out. I applied to the Institute of Education and bingo! The next thing I knew, I was doing a teaching course that would keep my fluency in my languages up to speed and I would also be able to give back to society by working with young minds. What a fabulous combination and way to use what I had learned.

I had dabbled with tutoring French and Spanish and even English during my year abroad but nothing on a grander scale.

Soon enough, I would be out in front of 30 lovely children. I had no idea really what I was in for.

6. Why Teach There?

'If you can teach here, you can teach anywhere.'

It was pandemonium with 10H. In the French class where I was supposed to gain all my wisdom and be shown how to teach, what I was observing was pure chaos. There were boys like those in class 10H everywhere – I suppose there would be, being a boy's school, but I mean everywhere.

Standing on the tables, running out of the classroom door in turns, even hiding under the teacher's desk at times, pulling pranks. The poor teacher, who I think was doing her best, was screaming at the top of her voice with cries of *'écoutez' and 'arrêtez' and 'asseyez-vous'* in her desperate urge to make them listen, comply and pay attention.

Oh, they were listening all right, and then plotting how they could make the decibels in her very large range reach the top of its scale. Not to mention that her style of dress included very light and airy flowing skirts which would get caught on the handle of her chair each time she rose from her desk. She would be in such a fluster she was totally oblivious to it so it would just rise up like a curtain between her newest 'away from desk' position to the desk. The desk under which a naughty Year 10 boy may have been sitting.

Notice I mentioned, each time she rose from her desk. Those of us in the know, know that desk-teaching is not the way it goes.

The key protagonist in this horror movie that I was watching was a boy called Dwayne.

I will never forget Dwayne. He was about four foot eleven. One of, if not, the shortest in the Year 10 group, but clearly the most deviant, naughty and influential of them all as the other boys looked up to him like some deity. I dreaded the thought of being the one, should I be given this class, to teach him. I made no attempts to linger my gaze whenever I watched him, ensuring he did not turn his maleficent ways towards me. Not necessarily because I was scared, but I was not sure if I would yet be in control of my 'Church Road' ways and just want to cuss this boy out, potentially damaging my chance at this whole teacher thing. It turned out there were about five Dwaynes at this school, all with poor behaviour, but this guy was by a long way the boss.

At this point, I am drawn to recall both from his presentation to university students in Zimbabwe and his book, *Natives*, Akala's note of significance that, during his school days in Camden, it was the norm that teachers would scan their list of names of students and predetermine the destiny of each child. It is a truth and still happens in some ways to this day.

By no means did it mean that every Dwayne I would henceforth encounter would replicate this particular student. However, Dwayne was, without doubt, a challenge, and no one seemed to be able, or have the passion to get to the crux of managing him to help him to learn. This was no fun. But who was I to complain? I had just begun a PGCE but, as a fledgling teacher, even though I had no experience, I knew this was not right. It was indeed totally wrong.

I think this is when my moral compass, or the birth of it, kicked in. These boys were getting a raw deal.

Meanwhile in the class next door, I could hear the bellowing, deep, gruffly pure French tones of the Head of Department. A six-foot large, imposing, twiddly-moustached and beard-wearing Caucasian French man with a booming voice who loved to sing. Looking back now, I realise why he had placed me in Ms Bartholomew's class twice a week, always when he was teaching across the corridor. Mr Latrelle had his Year 11 boys singing at the top of their voices, checking their pronunciation and diction. Intonation and passion were well-rehearsed alongside their vocal cords. It was quite something to watch.

Unfortunately, neither of the members of the department I was so desperate to learn the trade from inspired me to become the teacher I did. Mr Latrelle was of course much better and it would be remiss of me to say I didn't learn anything from him because I did – like not being afraid to make even the overgrown Year 11 boys engage in singing to support memory and retention of French. Fortunately, Mr Latrelle shared the class I had witnessed tormenting Ms Bartholomew so I was able to experience a more positive interaction with the boys when he taught them and I was attached to this group for those lessons as well.

I remember being told by our PGCE mentor in one of our sessions that we should not just stay within the confines of our departments but explore other subject areas. You did not need to ask me twice. The next day, I had plucked up the courage to walk around the school and just pop into lessons, asking politely if I could sit at the back and observe. That's when I discovered her, Ms Osborne. I should call her the 'goddess of teaching', Ms Osborne.

Her voice was calm, even melodic; she walked with poise and grace, she was uber-organised from start to finish, and had the boys eating out of the palm of her hand. Most impressive of all was the fact that in this class there were the almost identical group of students that were in Ms Bartholomew's class. They were unrecognisable. Once I was in this room, I planted myself at the back and watched the magic of Ms Osborne's history lesson unfold. 'Now THIS is the teacher I am going to model myself on,' I told myself.

That is exactly what I did. It didn't matter that her pedagogy was in a different subject. Pedagogy (the method and practice of delivering knowledge and skills in lessons), amazing behaviour management leading to the development of good secure relationships, coupled with good subject knowledge, are all the necessary ingredients you need to be a leader of your subject in the classroom; also a leader of teaching and learning, which I became when I went into senior leadership. More about that later.

Little did I know that Mr Latrelle planned to include 10H as one of the groups in my reduced timetable for teaching. I am sure that if you are a teacher you will relate to what I am about to say next. They told us on our PGCE course to never take the first register with your hand unsupported – in other words, without the support of the table or your other hand underneath it. Back in those days, the register was a wide green file. Everyone walked with a black and red pen. Black for absences that you would circle, and red to mark students as present. There I was, at the front of the classroom; I opened up my wide green register and then began to call the names out.

Damn! I had forgotten the advice and all of a sudden I had an out-of-body experience and saw my hand, poised above the wide green file, trembling furiously. Or so it seemed to me. Like a saviour, it flashed into my mind: 'keep your arm supported when you take the register in the early days', and I just ever so slowly lowered my hand down to meet the file and continued. It may seem trivial, but when you begin the teaching profession, everything matters. Everything continues to matter until you don't think of it anymore; then, you know you have mastered it. You have to, as Doug Lemov says in his book *Teach Like a Champion*, 'sweat the small stuff'. Although he is referring to whole-class teaching principles, I believe it also matters when developing as a teacher, as a group of 30 bustling boys can reduce you to nothing in a flash.

I made my way through my lesson, navigating the flashcards, on-the-spot marking and other strategies, and got to the plenary, the part when you summarise what they have all learned and get ready to send them on their way. All was going well, with a final feedback comment from Steve, a pause, and then Dwayne farted. It came from nowhere. I just paused in my tracks, pivoted and stared at the space in the classroom he occupied. Then I just glared. I said nothing. Neither did they. I could feel the sweat building up but I waited. It did me good. I pondered what my next move would be. There was a very tiny snigger. Dwayne was clearly testing the boundaries. But I had won. Some of the boys looked at me and quickly looked away, deciding whether to make this into something or not. I had not given them any ammunition and as a result it just fizzled away.

My fast heart rate didn't though. It was still going. My heart goes out to all beginner teachers. That's why I pledge never to forget my experiences of the early days. There are emotions galore – tiredness, self-doubt, anxiety, frustrations and more. The 'more' being moments of laughter, joy, funnies, special and yet more emotions but of a positive kind. I do believe it is one of the best careers in the world and maintain this today. As a headteacher, I can honestly say that this list of feelings never goes away, you just get better at knowing what to do with them. It's called experience.

From my experiences of teaching Dwayne and many others at Grampton High School, I realised I loved the challenge. I loved the possibilities before me of infusing my love of languages, and seeing the finished product. I got a buzz when, at the end of every lesson, I had made them listen, read, speak or even sing in French and I had shown them the fruits of their labour, that they could converse, and how this was just one tiny way the world was opening up for them.

I went from my first ever school in Harrow, Grampton High School for Boys, and took up a substantive role a month before I finished my PGCE teacher training. I had visited, managed to discuss with the Head of Department the potential of working there, and the next thing I knew, they were negotiating with Grampton and the Institute of Education how I could do my supply teacher role there a month before formally completing the course. I did it and was very glad for the opportunity.

I was 21 when I first set foot in the school. Only three years difference in age from the most senior students. I had to learn very quickly how to adopt my teacher-face and my 'don't mess with me' look. It was necessary, and it was the start of my behaviour management training. I began as a supply and also secured the substantive role as a teacher of French and Spanish.

This was not the expected subject for a teacher with my background or ethnicity. I remember the blue-eyed, blonde-haired David in my Year 10 French class who sat and stared at me for about 30 minutes. Every time I circulated to look at work, he would quickly look at his book to avoid eye contact and feign working. When I eventually asked, 'Is everything okay, David?' I think he just couldn't hold it any longer and blurted: 'Miss, you're our French teacher.'

'Yes, David, that's right. I am,' I replied, and paused.

'But you're black,' he said.

Bingo! Poor David, he had been tormented by this for the last half hour or so. But he had addressed the elephant in the room for the two of us. I knew that was what he was thinking all along and he just wanted the courage to talk about it.

This was when I really knew that I had crushed the stereotype of the 'French or Spanish teacher' and the image of what they should look like, or that all Black teachers taught English, Religious Education or Social Sciences in an effort to undo the injustices of racism and inequality. Not that this is in any way a less important area of education, not at all. I hold these subjects in very high regard and these teachers are responsible for the creation and inspiration of our much-needed social change agents. I had studied 'A' level Sociology myself but it highlighted the pigeon-holing that to some extent exists today. I have met a few Black Modern Foreign Languages or MFL teachers, most of them coming from outside the UK, and have only personally met one other teaching both French and Spanish like myself in all my career.

Wilkstone High School was a 15-minute walk from my home. It meant I was a teacher who was mingling with her students in the local area. I became the community mother. It wasn't without its turmoil and issues and one experience stands out for me. My big brother did not want me to teach at a local school. His previous school. I say it was the best decision I made.

It was one rainy afternoon when I came home and told him I had succeeded in getting the job at his previous school. He responded with 'Why teach there?' in sheer disgust.

One day when I came home early, I just broke down crying and I remember shouting at my brother, 'You don't understand. It's not that easy. You try controlling a class of 30 kids who don't know why it's important for them to learn!'

He replied with an 'I told you so!' and such antipathy that it led me to one reaction.

I became ever more determined to make a success of it. 'Thanks, John!'

Being as stubborn as I can be has given me dogged determination and a headstrong drive which drives my family, including my beloved husband, insane, but has contributed to my unblinkered focus and resolute determination to achieve things on my journey. If I could teach there, then I could probably teach anywhere.

Had I not been too upset, too tongue-tied and dumbstruck by his inability to see the potential of what I could do with these students, when my brother had asked me 'Why teach there?' I would have had a different answer.

It probably would have sounded something like this: 'I chose to teach there. Why not teach there? Who else can relate to the students in the way I can? Who will champion their cause, help them work through the despair of hope and limiting beliefs others hold of them, some of them their teachers?'

I was a member of, and loved, my community. I wanted to contribute in some way to it. If 'education is the passport to your future', then languages, my subject, were the passport to their world. I wanted them to have the opportunity to experience life outside the concrete jungle, even if that was through my eyes. Who else would have a shared understanding of their challenges, the peer pressure, the lingo, and not make them feel inferior and unimportant or misconstrue their street talk for something ridiculously different?

I loved that the students had character, that they would challenge me and they made me become a better teacher day by day. I had to differentiate so expertly in so many different ways. I got a real incomparable sense of satisfaction each time a parent would thank me for what I had been able to achieve with a language student or a member of my form.

The time I spent supporting the beginner learner of English who was really a Year 14, an 18-year-old, but had been put back a year. This student was able to relate and communicate with me, albeit in our broken Portuguese/Spanish creole. The young girl who had told me that she wanted to become a nurse. And in the same manner as Ms Simmonds, not only did I not react in surprise, I invited a friend of my sister's (she was in the medical field) to come and give a talk. I worked there even though I had refused to attend there as a student. I wanted to do better by them. I studied hard and worked through all my demons to become a teacher and I knew I was best placed, maybe not to study but to work there. This was where my purpose lay. These children needed champions and I could be one of them.

Following on from the challenges of the boisterous all-boys school, Wilkstone High gave me a superb foundation to teach at what was then one of the most challenging schools in England. If you want to test this, try Googling the names of the first wave of academies and why they were created in the first place. Wilkstone High School was the fourth school to be transformed into an Academy. It was transformed to Crown County Academy in September 2003, following the academies in the parliamentary constituencies of Hornsey and Wood Green who were first, followed by Middlesbrough and, thirdly, Camberwell and Peckham. Enough said. What Wilkstone High School provided for me was a great start to my teaching career.

I remember walking into the school building, the main entrance hall down the corridor to the left, when I saw the head of Physical Education rolling on the ground with a parent in a full-on fight. Apparently, this parent had disliked the sanction that had been imposed on their child. He wasn't accepting it and they both entered into fisticuffs as opposed to resolving the matter. I was only six months into the job. I did think, 'What if I impose a sanction the parent didn't like? How would they react then?'

Something in me made me hold my resolve. I was going to make a success of my position there.

From Hood to Headship

At Wilkstone High, my Head of Department gave me a small group with low ability to work with and support their literacy. Guess which name was on my list of boys? Yes, it was Dwayne. What a relief when he turned out to be a lovely, respectful, charming young man, dispelling the myth that children of a certain name are all bad. Many teachers will have a name or two they can recall with disdain, anguish or pain, having experienced a series of them in their careers. It is a strange phenomenon.

One of my early champions was Tobias Flemming, the headteacher of Wilkstone High at the time and who had been headmaster when my brother attended the school. Thanks to the legacy left by my brother who was a straight A* student, (grade A was beneath him) I think there was an expectation that I would be an 'academic' and maybe bring some of this to the school.

We must be careful as leaders and as teachers of doing the same with students, as we are all made of different stuff and I certainly was not my brother. That was probably a good thing; otherwise, the teacher army would have lost a fallen soldier.

I think Tobias did have great aspirations for me, however, and I was allowed to experiment, thrive and develop. This included me being thrown into the lions' den, looking after students in the 'remedial group' which became a winge fest for the most disadvantaged and underachieving groups in the cohort; a kind of 'sin bin'. I was not deterred but each day was thinking up ways to make this room a great experience and reverse the culture the students, mainly boys, had become stuck in. I definitely was not favoured, protected or given any dispensations. Wilkstone High School was a 'survival of the fittest' type of school and, if you couldn't hack it, you were gone in a matter of months. I am sure that Tobias was hoping I would stay for the long haul and grow with the school, contribute to replenishing the falling roll and perhaps one day take on the mantle of a senior post there, but as is normally the case, young teachers do move on. It didn't stop me from becoming a department second though, one year into the job, and I did work hard for it.

I grew in teacher maturity and expertise with my allocated form group, whom I also taught. An incident that remains in my memory was when one of the boys in my class came to the lesson late. It was an assessment and I was dictating what the students had to write.

His name was Alonso, the shortest boy in the year group. Alonso was a very special student. It was Alonso who stood up when I joined the school and was attempting to teach this crazy class, in which were three sets of twin boys, who were just running around like headless chickens during my covering of a Year 8 lesson. He shouted very loudly with his raw Jamaican accent: 'Unnu just shut up! Yu nuh see di teacher ah talk!'

The whole class just went silent. It was amazing and I was dumbfounded. From that day on, I had due respect from every student in that school, let alone just that class, all because 'bad bwoy Alonso', a reputation he had gained due to his extra-curricular activities, had stood in my stead and handled the class. It was a code for 'this teacher is all right'. I had passed his test, somehow. He had my back in a very strange kind of way because he had sensed and somehow knew, early on, that I loved what I was doing and I wanted the best for the students.

That was when he was in Year 8. We were now in Year 11 and Alonso had come into the class in a foul mood. I could see he was angry. I couldn't quite put my finger on it. As I approached him closely, continuing my dictation in Spanish to the class as they eagerly listened and made their attempts to have the best inscriptions, he slowly withdrew from his very washed-out, torn and tatty blazer, his pens, his highlighter (Miss Blankson (my maiden name) insisted on highlighters), his folded vocabulary notebook, his pencil case and his weed. I am sure he did this all with the aim of completing the test. His gaze, fixed at the edge of the desk. The moment he glimpsed upwards, I looked into his eyes. They were as red as hell fire. Then, unfortunately for him, the whiff of marijuana hit me. It was decision time. I could have gone stir crazy, I could have shouted, hauled him out, brought attention to the situation and maybe even tried to march him to the Head of Department or, worse still, the headteacher, but what would that do to help him?

The hours I had invested in supporting this boy in homework support after school, reasonings and challenging misconceptions. Building hope and aspirations, helping him to see the world was not against him as he argued his version of his truth, only to just drop him into a pit? Why? So, I leant close to him and simply whispered, 'Pick up your things and go home', at which point he looked at the table, recognised what he had put on it, then slowly, gingerly, recollected his belongings and disappeared. I infomed my Head of Department. It turned out his mum, who often travelled to Jamaica on business, was out again, and for sure every time mum had done that I was definitely her replacement, at least in school. Safeguarding as a term, did not even exist back then.

For at least an hour every day after school it was me and my boys, the most challenging boys in the school, reasoning, in Year 11. We talked about the elders and the injustices of their world. Why the world couldn't see their potential and allow them to be, and be fair to them, just like I was doing. Why the world did not treat them with honesty and dignity instead of pity or fear of them. We would talk and talk and sometimes it would go beyond an hour after school. Somehow, it helped them. I guess it made them come to school as they looked forward to that end of the daytime. Slowly the group grew from just four boys to six. Then a few of the girls joined as well. It was a sort of self-help group in the end.

The love of my job grew as I further developed a love for working with children and young people and it deepened my sense of moral purpose. By the time I was leaving Wilkstone High, I was taken out to a meal in Bayswater of all places, organised by the toughest of children in the Year 11 cohort, those who barely saw a good meal every evening themselves, many from single-parent and deprived households. It showed me that, given love, dedication and a true sense of care as we teach, the children will do anything for you.

As we bade goodbye to one another, one student, six-foot Shawn, athletically built, who was being raised by his mother on the Stonebridge estate, dodging the temptation to get into the life of gangs and dealing, a boy of usually very few words, stood over me and said, 'Miss, if you cry, you're not my teacher.'

I promised him, with eyes full of water, that I would not wail and attempted to not let the tear overflow onto my cheek. Susan handed me a tissue and it was all over. We laughed, hugged, and went our separate ways.

It definitely was not all laughs working at Wilkstone High School. I lost several students to the streets. One of the saddest days of my career was when my husband who worked for the organisation called 'Not Another Drop' – in other words, 'not another drop of blood', from the knife crime that was happening in the area – brought home the local newspaper. The front cover was dedicated to a march this organisation had instigated, dedicated to the fallen youths. As I looked at the faces on the front cover in remembrance of all those who had died at the hands of a knife or a gun, I began to pick off my students. It was heartbreaking seeing them all together. I was forced to remember the personalities, the potential, the lives cut short of every single one of them.

When I left, I moved to a girls' school. I had been so used to dealing with those from the school of hard knocks that my early encounters with poor behaviour left many of these students traumatised and I saw enough tears that could refill a bath in Nirvana Spa. I was simply too hard for this group of children and my style of discipline was not something they had experienced or were used to.

Whilst we might be thinking, 'This is great, I have no behaviour management problems to deal with then', the reality of having good classroom management is that happy children learn. I have learned that children are not ruled by fear. There will be those who can practise the art of articulation, freedom of expression and develop a voice, not through intimidation by adults, but by forming the teacher-student rapport built on a foundation of mutual respect. I had to soften, just a bit. Not too much that I couldn't handle the feisty American girl and her best friend, the only two who would have been a match for those at Wilkstone High, who stayed in my form the entire five years of her time there. She is a personal friend to this day. A protégée of mine. I kept my hard ways for them.

Success for my students looked like 80% A* – C each year for my GCSE students, and raising both the profile and the levels of attainment for all linguists who were entered for every language in which there existed a GCSE.

At this girls' school, worked one unique headteacher and three fellow deputies who brought a unique combination of strength, authority and demand. I couldn't believe it when, on my first day as Head of Department, I walked into the classroom where I was to hold my first department meeting. Inside sat the headteacher and one deputy head plus one other teacher. I was three years into teaching and I was expected to lead the headteacher and her deputy. They never told me this at the interview!

To this day, I hold that ex-headteacher and those deputy heads in very high regard. During my ten years at the school, not once did the headteacher or her deputy make me feel as though I did not know what I was doing. The headteacher had made a statement to me that, when she was in my meeting, it was my meeting. I had free rein to lead the team how I wanted to. I have to admit, I had a pretty clear vision of how I wanted this small modern language department to grow and flourish, and, boy, did I make that happen. I am eternally grateful to them for the leadership lessons I gained.

Firstly, let leaders lead. Micromanaging is not a good way to lead.

Secondly, coach a colleague rather than tell a colleague. Remember I said there was 'one other' – she proved to be a nightmare colleague to manage. My very first proper difficult conversation came via my dealings with her. She would do the opposite of what I asked, arrive late, leave early, refuse to contribute to the team, and argue with me in front of students. Suffering the affliction of the 'disease to please', I had battled for some time with trying not to pull rank, trying not to undermine her. I eventually learnt that I needed to breathe deeply, suck in my stomach and exclaim what I needed to and make my expectations known, even if it led to a full-on bust-up. After all, what could she do to me?

Finally, count on your experience. Having worked and supported even the most challenging of students to experience success, you know you have what it takes to coach, support and challenge others. As leaders we must do this, and drawing on whatever our experiences are can help us as we do.

7. Everyone Deserves a Champion

Rita Pierson in her TED talk (Pierson, 2013) raises awareness of every child needing a champion, and those who are disadvantaged most of all need this. It's called having agency. The higher up in your career the more you probably need the person in your corner, believe it or not, as the challenges to overcome become more covert. It's not cute as an adult to fail, get things wrong or laugh about your mishaps. The stakes are high and it can be a lonely place to deal with whatever goes wrong without at least one other who can have your back, offer some advice or encouragement as a means for you to carry on. I like to call them 'guardian angels'.

Providing agency, being an ally, or acting as a champion mean so much to me and I have found that the most competent leaders have all utilised the support or skill of those who fit in those camps. It is what emotionally intelligent people do. It is what conscientious people do too. For me, it is an aspect of career progression that all who have the privilege of moving up should be able to do as well.

I dedicate this chapter to the following identified champions without whom, I am pretty sure, the paths I took would have led me in different directions.

Ms Noel was my primary school form tutor. I was attending Stonebridge Primary School when I lost my mum. Ms Noel understood the importance of cultural capital. Cultural capital is the term that the English government decided to adopt from around 2018. Why did they take so long to realise that education is not just about the book and pen? The education of a whole child involves exposing them to a multitude of experiences.

My only question when I read about schools providing students with cultural capital is, 'From whose culture?' I imagine that, for the likes of our Prime Minister and his peers, it does not mean going to the Africa Centre or celebrating Pan Africanism or visiting a Caribbean restaurant, celebrating Kwanzaa, watching Black Heroes in the Hall of Fame at a local theatre or even attending the Notting Hill Carnival. For Ms Noel, it did. Their version of cultural capital would include a visit to a ballet or taking in an art piece at the National Gallery.

One day after school Ms Noel kept me and my friend Henrietta behind. She must have just felt so sorry for me and wanted to do something to relieve the look of sadness and anguish on my face after my loss. She told us we were going to go out with her and Miss Stevens.

That sunny afternoon she did take us to the theatre. The journey to Central London was very exciting because we took both the bus and Underground – the rumbling sound of which made me jump on the platform each time the tube arrived. We were taken to see *Ipi Tombi*. It doesn't exist now but anyone who has seen the play *Umoja* is likely to understand the spirit of this theatre piece. Back then, safeguarding looked like going above and beyond for a child without a second thought. I'm sure there must have been a phone conversation or a chat at the school gates on collection sometime prior, but Miss Noel just did what she felt she had to do and I will never forget the electrifying performances. Henrietta and I sang one of the songs for months afterwards. That was Miss Noel, looking after the bereaved, going above and beyond in extra-curricular.

Ms Simmonds was the next champion who spotted my leadership potential early on. She also recognised my singing abilities and I remember her being in one corner of the hall and putting me in the other and shouting 'sing!' so I would project my voice across the massive space in preparation for my role as Mary in the nativity. She also picked me for the captain of the netball team, even though it took me months to afford proper trainers to play in. She saw potential. This must have been my very first leadership role.

Janice Columbus was another role model. For her being the head did not mean you bullied your way around. Jan was a formidable, non-intrusive leader, allowing another leader to grow.

If someone had told me that I would be leading the headteacher and the deputy head at age 24 in a secondary school, I would have laughed. But that is exactly what happened when I joined the all-girls' school as a fledgling Head of Department.

In 2003, we had an exercise at school as part of a staff training day where we had to write down what we would be doing three years from then. I wrote, 'Hopefully, helping to develop other staff with CPD, providing training and maybe consulting on my areas of expertise.' More about this later.

Margarita Rufus told me she 'wanted me to experiment'. For a personality like mine, a stubborn sort who does not really like to be told what to do, this was music to my ears. I ran with it. She recognised effort and heart, and in her leadership style she modelled vulnerability. I remember a very sad occasion when we had lost a student to a terminal illness. As she walked up the stairs towards my office, she explained that she was popping in as she was checking in on all the senior leaders.

What began as a very calm and poised conversation took a change when, suddenly, she slumped into my chair and began to cry. She sobbed. At first, I didn't know what to do. This leader was at the top of the school and there she was in my office, bawling her eyes out, being completely in a zone of vulnerability. When she explained that she had felt like doing this crying for some time that day but only felt safe to do so in my office, it made me see the immense pressure of being a headteacher and how carrying this around must have felt for her. I was honoured that my office was the one where she could take off the mask and be her genuine, sincerely upset self. Why ever not? After all, we are all human.

This same individual had put me forward for the National Professional Qualification for Headship, otherwise referred to as the NPQH, in year two of senior leadership! She clearly saw my potential. Meanwhile, I ran a mile away from the idea!

If you are at a stage where you are doubting, considering the next step, making decisions, my advice would be to surround yourself with those who are just a little bit ahead of you. Take note of who your champions are or potentially could be. Consider how your connections can be useful and how you can learn and gain strength just from their existence, for no man is an island. It's important to also consider how you can be an ally to others. This has been said to be a critical aspect of networking for those who like to.

I'd like to end this chapter by highlighting two individuals who I am aware, that had it not been for them and their skilful intervention, care and attention as senior leaders, I probably would never have had the nerve to consider moving upwards at all. Two senior leaders who I worked with very closely and who were at the top of the school hierarchy. Throughout my time as a middle leader, I was able to shape, nurture and lead members of my department and they allowed me to flourish. My line management meetings were a meeting of two minds whenever I had them, and they were authentic, honest and open enough for me to feel that I could be the same. These two were pillars of strength when I finally decided to join the world of motherhood, as women can and will choose to do. Reaching out to me, never giving up on me when I was probably at the weakest point of my career, was a critical skill they demonstrated, and I am thankful to them both. Both were leaders with a mission to empower other women to feel as strong and certain as they did. They showed me the window to the world of motherhood, with all the amazing balancing acts of work and home life, before I had even thought about having my own children. Little did I know that I should have been taking notes from them, as this stage of my life was not easy at all.

8. Babies

'I used to have functioning brain cells and then I traded them in for children.' (Unknown)

It felt like wading through treacle. Each day, waking up at 4:00 a.m., getting the babies fed and dressed, and myself ready to leave at 6:00 a.m. certainly took its toll.

In 2005, I gave birth to my first son, Rahsaan Theo Kofi Manderson. Each one of his names meant something to me – my favourite jazz musician, his dad's legacy, Ghanaian heritage of Friday-born. How this bundle of new joy was going to change my life I had absolutely no idea. I remember feeling like I was on top of the world on his arrival, that I was 'made' and that I had accomplished the biggest achievement in my life, not merely because I had a completely natural birth. He came so quickly, by the time I had asked for gas and air, he was out. As the nurse put his warm soft body onto mine, he immediately latched onto my breast and started suckling. It was the most amazing feeling in the world. Wow, this little being was a true individual. It was hard to imagine he would turn out into a nearly six-foot man in the future. I turned to my husband Theo and whispered, 'Thank you.'

When I returned to work five months later, we had successfully achieved Language College status and finally the darkest and dingiest part of the school was going to be updated. I was lifting heavy boxes around as we prepared for our facelift and my colleague said, 'Are you sure you are okay to do this?'

I replied, 'Of course I am, I'm not pregnant, just tired.'

Six months later, I gave birth to my surprise, Isaiah Levi Kweku Manderson, who decided he was coming whether I liked it or not.

Sure enough, two months after giving birth the first time, I had conceived again, much to my chagrin. I had not planned this one!

It was not according to my plan. You see, those who know me know that I am a bit of a control freak. I like to have tick sheets and timelines. Intending to continue to exude my superpowers of middle leadership, I had planned every single day of my first maternity leave and even the exact amount of money I would earn over the period, down to the penny. I knew when I would return to work and resume my high-profile Borough Languages Lead role, as well as upgrade our Modern Foreign Language department further, to achieve our new specialist status; that alone had taken three attempts.

Prior to Isaiah's arrival, for the umpteenth time I dragged myself out of bed, tired as hell. The kind of tired where your limbs feel like 20 stones each and your gut cramps, twists and turns as you muster all the deep-seated essence of energy you can, just to move. It was a rainy morning in October. I stumbled and clobbered my way, like a beast out of a Frankenstein film, into the bathroom with my overgrown belly. Not a toe in sight! I trod painstakingly, sluggishly, as I looked down to ensure I was putting one foot in front of the other. I went through the motions of somehow enrobing myself with attire. I even managed to put some eyebrow pencil on. There was no way I would attempt a face of make-up. My skin had darkened anyway, and it looked ghost-like on my face. I eventually walked outside to my car. I ran through in my mind the menu of the day, the classes I would have and especially, the students, the ones I wanted to target for the day in class 10c1. I had promised Carleen I would go over the preterite tense just for her this time, and it was first period. Very slowly, I opened the passenger door, as usual. I slumped my school bag onto the seat, as usual. I closed the door as usual. I walked, well, waddled, to the driver's side, as usual. I heaved myself into the car and sat in the driver's seat, as usual. As the mist descended over my eyes, I fumbled around in my jacket pocket, pulled out my keys and put the key into the ignition, as usual. And then, it happened. I broke down. My legs and arms just froze. Why was this happening? I needed to get to school! I had things to do. My desk was messy because I said I would go back in early and tidy up before the day. Carleen was relying on me, she needed me. Nothing moved me. How could this be happening? I told myself, 'I am a competent superwoman, with a child now. I am strong. I am worthy. I am capab ... '

I just couldn't. I slumped over the steering wheel and I started to cry. I sobbed, uncontrollably. I just could not move. Theo had already left for work. It was about 6:30 a.m., I was not about to call anyone. I don't think I would have been able to see any digits if I had tried.

It must have been an hour or two later when I had finally calmed down and called my sister who came to the rescue. I sat in the car, her in the passenger seat next to me, speaking to my colleagues to explain that I was unwell and would not be coming in to work that day. I didn't return for a year.

Post-natal depression is not a joke. Even just writing those words fills me with emotion still. It is real. However, back in the day, there were not so many help groups, and being a teacher I was not used to being so open and vulnerable. We are the ones usually being there for so many others. Therefore, the thought of letting someone know: I was struggling; that my limbs felt heavy; my eyes felt like they were closed; and I couldn't see the wood for the trees, let alone remember what lessons I had each day and deliver them, was not something I was about to do any day soon. So, I suffered in silence, until I imploded. Just the thought of having this experience would go on to haunt me, even though I eventually came through it, thanks to the incredible support of some key friends and family.

It is not a place I would ever want to visit again nor want for anyone else. I now know and recognise that a lot of the depression did not stem from a lack of planning, or even the financial worries we were encountering, but from anger. I was angry that I had to work so hard, angry that my body had to undergo the changes it did, and angry that I had not accepted that this would simply be different. Being a planner, I was angry that I had not planned to be flexible enough to manage it.

Two years later, I found myself standing at the board. Standing in front of my most treasured bunch of students in the all-girls secondary school who were so excited that their form tutor and teacher of languages had returned. I had agreed with the deputy head that it could be an observation, just to check in that I had not lost my touch and that I could still teach.

The moment had come and, based on my prior experience and expert skills at delivery of modern languages with a bunch of uninterested, cockney-laden, estate-living teens, she had asked if she could have the visiting local authority bod observe with her. I agreed.

Big mistake. I stood at the board, my extra-large board I had installed with the interactive one as part of my gift to myself as the Head of Department and part gift to the school for achieving Language College Status two years before. As I raised my hand to write my first words with the whiteboard pen, I suddenly needed to ask myself the most stupid question: 'Where do I write the date again?' It was downhill from there. Baby brain.

All had been wiped away, including the simple routine of how I began my lessons. I had spent years crafting a system and a rhythm, starting from the way I laid out my tasks using the board, down to exactly how and when students participated, and then celebrated their achievements at the end of every lesson. Even the most defiant and staunch girl's attitude did not phase me. After all, I was from the 'ends' and I was just as feisty and quick-mouthed as the best of them. I had a strategy that forced them to learn, and learn they did. That day, I had failed. I could not believe that it had all gone. I felt so lost.

Had it really been that long? Had I really lost my touch? Indeed I had and, from the other end of the classroom, I could see the deputy head's face of shame, shock and embarrassment, of and for me. I was so scared from that moment on, I was almost literally 'shitting myself'. I am sure a few farts escaped as a result. Resilience is not just a word, it is a state of action and I needed to recover. I closed my eyes for a moment. I inhaled deeply, I visualised, not a top grade 1 but a grade 3 in the knowledge that I was not my former self. I knew there would be work to do. Never in my teaching career had I performed as a sub-standard or less than 'outstanding' teacher till now. First time for everything?

Okay, but being the kind of person who aims for perfection and usually almost gets it, I fell, very hard. It was a good lesson in imperfect perfectness and how to never underestimate the level of skills and knowledge acquired, which had been lost. It is important to always refresh.

Most of all, I regretted not keeping in contact. A phrase I learned about as maternity leave information changed, and along with it came the concept of 'keeping in touch' (KIT) days.

My advice to all new mothers: make the most of KIT days. I would consider: coming into school; reorienting myself around the buildings, the corridors, the playgrounds, the noise; completing small tasks from home and returning for short meetings to discuss them. Oh, and don't forget your classroom and that all-important board or screen. In a school, it might be for marking meetings or sharing your plans for a new scheme of learning, for example. You might decide to go to school to participate in whole school professional development days or, if you prefer a smaller scale, just in your department. KIT days are there. Use them. Don't assume all will be well on return after having your children.

I was very fortunate that the deputy head and I had worked so closely together. She had every faith in me returning to my former amazing self and so did the rest of the team. There was little convincing she had to do to tell me to up my game so I would not be subjected to increased monitoring or even capability. I was fortunate, as I know this is not the case for many in some schools.

As a headteacher, I have had seven maternity and two paternity leaves in my first year. Whilst this is expensive to the school and disrupts the constitution of the teaching population temporarily, the payback in terms of these colleagues' input, during and after their maternity or paternity leave, has been immeasurable. Keeping in touch, knowing their needs, ensuring they are supported upon return is vital. One deputy head's letter, sent by Royal Mail to my home during my period of depression, is a constant reminder to me of this to this day. It's no wonder she won the *TES* Headteacher of the Year some years later.

My children are my world. These two boys, whom I likened to baby cubs after seeing them play-fight on my sofas, destroy furniture, that needed to be taken for walks where they would even play 'fetch' when I threw the ball, had taught me a huge lesson in motherhood. I was a new mother, but I was still Miriam, the friend, sister, teacher, mentor, Head of Department, and all the other facets I had developed into my character over the years, in addition to being 'mummy'.

Babies.

Sixteen years later, as I write this, I can laugh at it all. But babies grow and change, and so do we.

Having children was life-changing for me. I went through the whole post-natal depression (PND) and, to top it off, my husband and I were struggling financially. Especially when the second child came, as the childcare fees were astronomical. People out there should prepare us better for these things! It got so bad at one point, our separate meals of breakfast, lunch and dinner became the luxurious uni-meal of tuna and rice with the odd replacement of dumpling for breakfast, just for a bit of variety.

This was when the feelings of self-doubt and thoughts of being a failure probably began to really fester. Children make you re-evaluate your existence and your worth. It took a lot of stomach-tightening resilience to overcome the negative thought processes I was constantly battling, as well as my efforts not to feel resentful at my husband for not being a wealthy individual which would have alleviated my feeling this way.

At the same time, this stomach-tightening came when I did not want to speak or act in a way that would make him see my frustrations or make him feel at fault. I was aware of the need to uplift my man, not destroy him, not damage the male ego. The inability to get up and do what I wanted to do, to think of my needs, was really difficult to overcome. In the end, it took me seven years to yield and finally accept that this was the new life for me.

In those seven years, I started my first ever blog. This was my first attempt at blogging many moons ago and this is the story that led me to journal my thoughts. It's a tricky thing, especially when it concerns work, as you don't quite know how much to keep in your head and how much to get it out! It is very necessary at times to clear your head but it still requires 'caution'.

Well, as I was preparing dinner for the family in the kitchen, I wrote my first entry and had selected the image of the mother cooking whilst on her laptop at the same time. My then five-year-old first-born, looking at the picture, asked, 'Mummy, can you do those two things, at once?' It made me laugh. I felt like exclaiming, 'Aren't I doing that now?' Seems it went unnoticed unless it was in a picture form, I guess.

My hubby had told me about a lady who had written a blog about the secrecy of breaking virginity and how successful her blog became; not that I wanted to go into that specialism. Realising that her blog became a great book made me think about the opportunity. Yes, I hear you. 'So, you think that will happen to you?' 'Er, no, not exactly. It wouldn't be a bad thing though!' (I think).

It's just that I figured I would write and air my views, complaints, frustrations, loves and laughs in a blog format and share it. I wasn't exactly sure. One certain thing was it could end up being quite therapeutic and save my hubby's ears from my complaining of the battles I was having, such as the one that led me to start this thing called blogging.

So it all kicked off with my work. You see, being an assistant headteacher in a secondary school has its challenges. Of course, not the school kids. No, more like that work-life balance thing. I had been asked to attend a residential with the senior leadership team (SLT) and my son had been taken ill. I had written to express my leave from the event and given my reasons, without considering that this might be refused. After all, what could be more important to a mother than an unwell child?

Boy, was I wrong. It felt like I had my priorities wrong in the eyes of others. I couldn't believe it. How could I not want to spend time with my sick child, who had chickenpox? Despite this, I was asked to come into work, and was told 'It is the worst time you could be off!'

'Helloooooo! Which part of "sick child" did you not read in my communication?' I thought.

My journal entry read:

> *Let me see, sick child... work... sick child... work... sick child... yes, that's the one that resonated with me most.*
>
> *It was time for our team to have a residential with good quality thinking time and, of course, good old hubby had already taken time off to be with our kids so I could pursue my work and career yet again. In spite of this, I was again given emails making it clear that my wanting to be at home with a sick child was not good enough in favour of spending quality time and 'bonding' time with my colleagues (by the way who I would see a total of 40 hours at least per week! – While I saw my sons possibly ... wait for it... 40 hours a week, on a good week (not counting sleeping – eyes are closed so not seeing them! Just in case you wanted to be pedantic).*

Nevertheless, the bit about being 'one of the most able, and reliable members of the team' did influence me, if I'm honest. Call it emotional blackmailing of sorts, or knowing my value, of recognising worth, and the importance of being accredited would make me second guess. So, off I went the very next day to work, to this event, despite a night of broken sleep. I had had about three hours in total of any sleep and felt extremely tired, menstrually fatigued, and challenged.

This just made me mad! Being the good soldier I am, I did everything in good stead. The result: work carried on as it should. The more serious implication, however, was that my hubby's life was not important enough or even considered, never mind the kids. Then again, why would anyone else care but me? So, I needed to make a stand, be bold, next time.

This was a good revelation of my values. In this case, the value of family. You see, our decisions are always fuelled by our values. It is what keeps us authentic but also highlights if we have another value which is courage.

At this point, I did not have the courage to put my foot down and say I would not yield to the requests, especially if I was such a reliable and worthy colleague, then some of the give back should be allowing time to tend to what I feel is important. That was then.

Now, I would have a different response and I think many in society have come away from the 'martyr' parent thinking and do put their feet down. It takes courage to do this, be convicted. As a headteacher, as one of my values I am always careful about what impact my decisions over such requests will have on the individuals and long-term on the institution. If you want to get great gains, it is important to know the worth of the staff. I believe the more you give the more you get back. The balance is in ensuring you are not always giving and others taking liberties.

I named my blog 'The Mumventures of Bionic Woman'. Why that title? you may ask. When I was a little girl, I had an aunt who called me Bionic Woman. This aunt even bought me the catsuit which I wore all the time with pride, as I loved it, until there were holes in the crutch and sleeves.

Image taken from *https://twitter.com/missymanderson/photo*

Now, many years later, I think to myself that she must have been prophetic. Although I don't feel like I'm quite the Bionic Woman of the 1980s, it did feel like I strove to be, pretended to be, or somehow felt I needed to be 'Bionic Woman'. *I'm not Wonder Woman but God made me Wonderful (Walsh, 2008).* This is the name of one of the books I read at this time. I chose it because the title jumped out at me when I tried to regain my passion for reading. The challenge was if I could restart this passion, I would be finding myself some 'me time' successfully.

It was awesome. Here, in the words littered all over the white pages, was an author who also experienced the superhero-becomes-mum syndrome. I think there are many of us out there. A bit like the X-Men, we are the 'mutants' walking around in recognition of one another, coming from a secret world that only those of us going through it are witness to the evidence.

In my blog I had written: 'I'm not an author, although I would love to be. As a senior leader in a big comprehensive secondary school, who has dabbled in the music industry, a Christian mother who works long hours, like other bloggers, I just want a space to air my thoughts aloud so I hope you enjoy reading.' The real reason behind its conception though came from a lesson in leadership.

In 2013 I read *'I'm no Wonder Woman but God Made Me Wonderful'* (Walsh, 2008). What a wonderful read it was. It was the essence of me. A Christian woman, contending with the 'wannabe superhero' syndrome. Super mum, super wife, super colleague, super sister, super lover, super everything-to-everyone. Sheila Walsh presented me with some real nuggets around my feelings of self-esteem, anger, fear and wearing of masks, capes and boots. How I wished I had discovered her book sooner.

Being mentally ill did not stop me from being successful and it would be worth anyone reading this to make a note. Be they the ones who have suffered from mental illness or those who judge others when they do. The organisations we work in can play a big part in how well mothering staff recover and regain their mojo after they have had it knocked out of them by childbearing or adopting.

I will be eternally grateful for the senior leaders at the school I was at who exercised patience and ardent optimism in my ability to get myself back!

Image: iStock.com/ Svetlana Barmina

Part 2

The Only Way is Up!

9. New to Senior Leadership

'If two of us are the same, that makes one of us unnecessary. Be an individual, be your authentic self.'
(Adapted quote from Larry Dixon)

The phone rang. I let it ring. I had hoped it would ring out. Eventually, I decided to pick it up.
'Hello, is that Miriam Manderson?' the voice said.
'Yes, speaking,' I returned.
'Oh hello, this is Suzanne Smith from St Christopher's School – we would really like you to reconsider joining us. I promised to call you again to see if you would rethink and accept the job offer?'
I paused. 'Were they for real?' I thought.

This was the third time they had called. I had said on the day that this was probably not going to work for me and I would not be taking the job. They had rung and checked and checked again.

'I am so honoured that you have called me back again but I have had a rethink and also discussed this with my husband and I do feel I am making the right decision. I am afraid I won't be taking the job offer on this occasion, but thank you once again for calling me.'

I knew then, the only way was up.

I had been battling with the shock to my system of motherhood; the return to my former self was taking longer than I had anticipated. The dark days were turning to light, but I really regretted not taking up the KIT days. KIT stands for 'keeping in touch' to help mothers remember what the hell they did before childbirth. I had three options: apply to do the Future Leaders programme, an expedited route to headship where they expected you to become a head within two years of finishing the course; apply for a senior leadership role in a school closer to home (it would cut an hour from my daily drives), as a means to progress and challenge myself further to speed up my development; or, to reconsider it all and go for a less demanding role.

It would be a step backwards, to come out of leadership entirely and be the second in charge of a department. I hoped it would help me regain a work-life balance. I acted on all three options.

As my application forms sat in the offices of the secondary school I had applied to for an assistant head role and the office of the then Future Leaders administration, there I was refusing the job offer I had received for the deputy Head of Department job. The backward step. My husband had told me that I couldn't do this job because I would be bored in two minutes, and working under a middle leader whose values might not align with my own, but did I listen? No. Which wife does? I had to go through this and see for myself.

The truth is, what sealed the decision was the Head of Department's response that there would be 'no displays on the walls' and 'everything was decided by her'.

'Later!' my younger self had said, not out loud of course. 'Seriously?'

Instantly, I was switched off. I mean, I am a modern languages teacher by trade, displays for British children learning foreign languages are a no-brainer and an absolute must.

I could already sense that this would be a battle of the leaders/ex-leader versus current leader, and I would of course win, but I had my personal fight already – babies versus 'mummy monster', the term my boys had resorted to naming me. Apparently, I was the punching bag and I wasn't about to bring her into the ring too. So that was it. Decision made. I can't lie about how it made me feel needed. The school wanted me. They could see my value. I knew then, I had not lost it all and that I had begun my escape from the mental confinement that had held me captive – baby brain, lost sense of self, and diminished confidence.

I said to myself, 'Okay, girl, the only way is up. Let's try going towards senior leadership.'

What I didn't realise then was that, having never fathomed the idea of leading a school, I would someday be applying to be the headteacher of one. Other people seemed to have more confidence in me than I could muster in myself. I recall writing an entry in my OneNote. It was on Tuesday 19 July 2016 at 00:06 a.m. It was entry number 16, simply entitled as a quote from what this colleague had said: **'When you're head'**. The entry read:

> *Those words resonated with me when a colleague told me today that they would return but only if I were the head. I still can't understand how some colleagues have faith in me or see what they see in me. I don't see it myself although I am aspiring, I don't believe that anybody else has the same aspirations as I do for myself and I struggle to see myself believing that I still have a long way to go, lots of knowledge to*

learn, lots of things to experience, lots of solutions to find the problems to, and really prove that I am worth my weight in gold.

In 2005 when I returned for the short time from maternity leave number one, in an activity at a whole staff morning briefing, we were made to write where we saw ourselves in three years. I had written 'as a developer of people, something to do with training others, sharing experiences and skills across a wider breadth of people'.

Three years later, in 2008 I was successfully appointed as an assistant headteacher for staff development and performance.

Never underestimate the power of visualisation and of writing down your goals.

How awesome. My children were two and three years old. One was still not sleeping right through the night so I had suffered severe sleep deprivation but the light at the end of the tunnel shone on the new fact that I would now be working closer to home and not travelling the three hours I did every day. I would still need to change over cars at our checkpoint, the nursery, as my husband and I swapped to exchange our loot (the boys in their car seats) and he drove off to do the night shifts he was doing as I sleepily drove home. We were like ships in the night.

I was so excited to be going into senior leadership that I began to stay awake past that dreaded crossroads I came to midway through my journey home. Usually, I would be startled awake by honking horns as I had fallen asleep at the lights and looked around to see annoyed drivers behind me who were infuriated as I had caused them to miss and wait for the next sequence of the traffic light changes. Oops! Now, behind the wheel, I imagined what I might be doing, I conjured up how I would shape staff professional development plans and it kept me motivated and awake on my drives until I began one term later, in the autumn of 2008.

It was not easy. I had taken over from a colleague who had been diagnosed with a terminal illness and I didn't know that she was who I had been appointed to replace. Uber-awkward! I found out by chance in a conversation I was included in when the colleagues assumed I had been told. The problem was, she was also in the room! From that moment on, I felt very uncomfortable. Every strategy I thought up seemed to be rubbished. On reflection, could it have been constructive criticism that was sharpening my focus? Each colleague I liaised with seemed to have already been intercepted by this colleague. Whenever I approached a colleague, she had already met with them and planned my strategies. I felt as though I was stepping on someone else's toes but in fact, on reflection, she was stepping on my toes. This was my job!

In my mind, I perceived looks of indifference when I handed out discussion papers to the team or when presenting my ideas and my plans for the development of the entire staff body. I didn't know how much gravitas this colleague had but I soon learnt. Until I had felt the temperature of the school, it appeared it was already a threat to my stability. Could this have just been conjured up in my imagination and due to my already destabilised sense of worth I had arrived with? Possibly and possibly not. The leadership team was, let's say, very experienced and between them probably had a total of 500 years of age. I joined as the youngest member of this leadership team and I was often reminded of it in various ways. Life in senior leadership had begun and I totally stepped up to the challenge.

Life as a senior leader showed up as a lot of work.

Scratch that.

It showed up as an immense amount of work.

It seemed to be incessant and came from everyone above, sideways and below. To make matters worse, I remember feeling really out of my depth from the first day when I had to plan an induction for new staff, but I had not been inducted myself! Let me tell you, it was the speediest and most intense induction in history as I swallowed all the documentation I could and learnt as many facts about the school as possible because I wanted to be in a position to lead, model and direct others from a position of knowledge and confidence.

The different jobs include line managing middle leaders, an enormous amount of reading to keep abreast of current educational policy, analysing data, creating reports, planning improvement strategies and the almighty pressure of making decisions, not to mention a dose of disciplining or being a bodyguard when the need arises. Fundamentally, a senior leader is critical in setting the tone of the establishment, the culture and the ethos. It is definitely not a 9:00 a.m.–5:00 p.m. job, and cannot be done in the school day, leaving copious amounts of work that steal parts of home life. Anything can happen, as no two days are ever the same. Striving to achieve a work/life balance became my mission and drove me to a fabulous book called simply *Busy,* by Tony Crabbe. It was a game-changer.

Sometimes I think that I was probably being dumped on but in my ignorance, newness and with my desire and efforts to please, I wanted to show my abilities and prove my worth as a senior leader so I took it all on.

When I started senior leadership, I began writing my 'SLT Tales', journaling over the years in my online portfolio from **Blue Sky Education** and one example of how I found the challenge in the jump-in workload is the entry below:

Return from Tonsillitis! Again!!!

10 Feb 2010

How much role modelling can the SLT do when their desks are overloaded with tasks that seem insurmountable and they look tired!!! February has brought the dawn of the 'whoa' feeling onto all as I speak with my colleagues. My body just caved in I think and I gave in to the virus once again. I'm back but literally on 'shaky' ground with my legs still feeling jelly-like as I walk calmly around the school, seeming in control when in actual fact I am making sure I get to my destination and am juggling the 50 jobs in my head, which shall I do first? Well, without having even finished the book by Stephen Covey I began about 6 years ago! I have adopted the four areas and filed my papers into them for a start: important and urgent, not important but urgent, urgent but not important, and not important nor urgent. Let's see how that goes. Now I have governors till whatever time this evening, starts at six and I must get on and read a bit about it in preparation. So many documents to get through...

This was the sound of me grappling with becoming a senior leader. No one told you how to prepare and no one really could. Not then anyway. Now there are National Professional Qualifications for Senior Leadership and Aspiring to Senior

Leadership courses of every kind. Every school and every context brings with it its unique surprises, making it impossible to predict and plan for each one. The jump from serving 10 years as a middle leader, where I could run my department with my eyes closed and one hand behind my back as I orchestrated learning both within and outside of the classroom and even managed behaviour in my multilingual way, was more than I had imagined. When I sat in an Ofsted Shadowing programme conference, the facilitator said, 'you always go for jobs you have not yet done, but in them, you will grow'. How right he was.

Especially in this profession, applying for the next step means 'I will prove myself in the job when I get there'. Usually, in education, you have not done the role before. You don't get to do an episode of 'Faking It', a run-through or rehearsal, before you are officially given the role. So, it's important to imagine yourself already there, and create opportunities you may find to give yourself the heads-up in areas you are unlikely to get experience in from your current position.

You may have observed someone in the position and even thought to yourself sometimes 'I can do that', but walking in their shoes brings a different perspective. Add on the personal emotions and historical experiences which may impact feelings and level of self-belief and you have a fresh new situation to deal with.

Professional development plays a key role in confidence-building if you select the appropriate courses or use the appropriate channels to engage in them. When I was asked to do the NPQH in my second year as a member of SLT, I saw myself as a very small fish in a very large pond. I didn't feel anywhere near ready to embark on this. Little did I know how empowering this programme would be. All things in their time. I was never in a hurry to reach the top, just passionate about honing my craft of teaching and leading.

On days like this, the sense of seniority can reign and give us the means to go on, but it was hard. When I made it into the senior leadership team at the new school, I was consciously aware that I was not only young but the youngest in the entire team of 13. I also felt as though members of the team looked at me and said to themselves, 'What can she know? – she is so young.'

I was young in comparison to the others who had a seat at the large round table, others in my equivalent role who showed the wear and tear and seasoned look of wisdom perhaps and a bit more age.

When these thoughts arose, I used to revoke them with my counter-thought: 'This does not stop other very young senior leaders who don't care about the lack of experience they hold, so why should it stop me?'

My self-talk took on a life of its own. It used to jump out of my head and look me in the face with a threat – 'You'd better shape up or ship out. You did not work your way up from the concrete jungle to give in – so what's it gonna be?'

10. Doing Leadership in My Style

Senior leadership entails a massive amount of administrative work, heaps of reading, analysis, planning and decision-making. In most schools, unless you are the head, you are still managing it all with a teaching timetable, so you still have the planning, preparation and marking, parents' evenings and any other conversations with other adults as and when the need arises. You also need to be 'on call' at any moment in a school which can mean incessant interruptions – usually, just when you are getting into a flow. It means that much of what you begin gets finished in the hours you steal from your home life. It's just the way it is in the vocation of teaching.

During the school day, you also have to skilfully manage whatever urgent situation arises that you are on call for.

Relationships with all colleagues must remain professional and that can involve plenty of deep breathing and lip biting as you use a nanosecond to plan your next moves.

Whenever such situations arise, you can imagine how embarrassing it is for a senior leader to be called and it turns out to be the very individual with whom there may be some divergence. Having the bigger picture for school improvement means at times you see things differently. Middle leaders, rightly so, fight to protect their department's interests but it can lead to disappointments and even retraction, and disintegrate to improper and unprofessional behaviours.

An occasion like this happened when I rescued a colleague from a student whose skin she had gotten under so much that they had taken the fire extinguisher and threatened to hurl it somewhere. When I arrived at the class, I saw the blood had drained from the teacher's face; she clearly needed help and it could only come from me at that time, being the nearest senior leader on hand to help, but also the one who was not in her list of 'favourites' at the time.

Later, she admitted (not to me) that a big piece of humble pie was served to her as I skilfully and calmly diffused the situation and walked the student out of her class. What she learnt from this, however, was how I had modelled a conversation with a student that could abate instead of provoking an adolescent to the point of desperate fury.

The initiation rites on joining this new team were to line manage perceptibly the most challenging middle leader in the school, unbeknown to me. I found out much later that the attempted line management of this colleague had failed miserably by a succession of other senior leaders, including the head! This colleague had been rotated around. As a middle leader, you are used to having a member of the SLT line manage you. You move from being line managed to line managing. There is no rule book, so you are likely to have learnt from whatever has worked with you or what you have observed. I did my best, combining the best of what I had gained from the three brilliant line managers I had previously, and using leadership styles in my own carved-out way.

What hurt me most of all about this colleague and added to the revelation of my naïve self, was it was a 'sista'. A fellow member of the Black African or Black Caribbean community. UK Black, in my neck of the woods, had eventually accepted our joint fate and we had a more homogenised acceptance of our united front.

I was bitterly disappointed at the lack of vision, complete refusal to take responsibility for anything of this colleague, their vanishing drive and, most of all, the oxymoron of being a person who held very high qualification status and very high educational competence. Unfortunately, my perception saw a total and abysmal lack of love for, and understanding of, children.

Let's just say that every time I went into a line management meeting, I had to pull out the armour and go into battle. It got so bad one day that this individual dared to slap a piece of paper out of my hand and, in doing so, slapped my hand!

You can only imagine how a girl like me, from 'the ends', had to reign in all the 'Churchroadness' in me and muster all the decorum within me I could, to just stand up, and request that they leave my office. It was an ongoing saga. I remember feeling totally disappointed and internally conflicted as I had wanted so badly to see an example of excellence.

I am sure I am not alone when I state that, when it comes to others who may look like me, I only have good wishes for them. If they are a colleague, I want to feel proud of them. I am optimistic that they will shatter any existent stereotypes of being less competent, lazy, defensive or aggressive – a term some of us have come to hear overused. What we do not hope to experience is a perpetuation of all the above. It crushed my spirit that I was unable to champion the work output as it simply did not 'cut the mustard'. It's difficult to do whenever performance is embarrassing and cringe-worthy at times.

In the Black community, when someone leaves the 'hood' or seems to progress upwards, there are times when that individual has to bear the brunt of another's frustrations. It is not an uncommon story to hear. They believed that somehow, because someone has progressed or holds a superior position, they think of themselves more highly than others. Individuals who make it out of the 'ghetto' or 'hood' can become the subject of these charges for no reason at all, other than a presumption. It is a sad phenomenon. There have been times when, no matter what I have said or done, I have still had to contend with a standoffish reception.

Eventually, you decide to just stop trying to meet people halfway, or continue to put out olive branches and make peace. After all, shouldn't we have been looking out for each other, uplifting one another? The common denominator of years of oppression, continued misfortune, and the predominant subject of children and families facing disadvantage, including racism, over the years, has held us back. This should bind us together to support the community to do well.

'To build and maintain our community together and to make our brother's and sister's problems our problems, and to solve them together.'

Isn't this in the spirit of the Kwanzaa principle of Ujima?

Well, that was my understanding. Birds of a feather stick together, right? 'Each one, teach one'? Sadly, there are those of the flock who refuse to buy into this adage, even though I want to bring others along.

Image: iStock.com/katflare

I can truly say I gained two things from this early experience of line management, one positive and one negative: the ability to have difficult conversations, and high blood pressure.

It was not until having to go through many palavers and experiences of early line management that I had my true breakthrough moments. Given that I had been purposely committed to my professional development throughout my career and especially as a middle leader, with completion of courses such as 'Leading from the Middle', you would think that I would have had my 'turning point' or, as they called it, my 'learning breakthrough' during this time. Well, no. It took me an academic year and three months for the real breakthrough to happen.

My enlightenment came from a combination of this, as well as reading the book *New to the Senior Leadership Team* from my new Senior Leaders union, ASCL. My breakthrough highlighted the importance of leading through the empowerment of others. I remember telling my headteacher that I had learnt the most in a single week in February, that it was a serious learning curve, and that I had experienced a lightbulb moment that made me say out aloud: 'This is leadership.'

Reading the book confirmed a few things I saw in myself. Firstly, that I suffered from the curse of the 'disease to please'. Secondly, it is normal to feel like the new kid on the block, wanting to get things right, fit in at the right times, and yet get to know a new culture as quickly as possible by asking searching questions, navigating around, all the while knowing that you are under the watchful eyes of everyone, sizing you up, seeing how you handle things. Something that never stops as a leader.

As inadequate as I felt sometimes, it was a good way to remember that I had been employed as a result of the qualities that I demonstrated in the interview, but once in the post, it becomes easy to push this aside and forget. It becomes easier to forget your priorities and do what others want you to do and forget that you can define, or re-define as in my case, the role you are given – in my case, the professional development coordinator, director of staff development and performance. My predecessor eventually left the school and I had full reign of my area.

Line management is not all challenging and enduring difficulties though. It is about working with and through others. A breath of fresh air was managing one of the most gentle, humble, and emotionally intelligent leaders in the school.

My competition came from inside, the head of a successful subject department. I didn't expect to get the role, given that this Head of Department was revered and loved by his team. When I realised I had succeeded against an internal candidate, it boosted my self-esteem, but only for a minute. The demands of the role made me question if I had taken on more than I could chew. I then felt the pressure of being the line manager. Yes, I was given the task of managing him.

All I can say is I must have been a decent manager as we developed the kind of peer-to-peer congeniality, with regular dialogue, based on mutual respect and a shared mission to do right by the students at the school. I learnt as much from him as he did from me. True leaders know this accounts for 50% of success.

As I grew into my role, leadership in my mind meant taking the back seat more than the front and allowing your colleagues to flourish, although some can see they will either sink or swim. Some we lead will rise to the challenges presented to them whilst others want to cling to support; some can be very needy.

One of the skills I needed to develop is that of letting go, not getting too involved and really demonstrating the ability to be an impartial leader. My view of what a leader is has guided my behaviour and the way I view how others view me. My belief that a leader should be 'good at everything', even though I know this is untrue, has been a common thread in the way I have thought, reflected, felt, and even responded in certain situations.

In that very demanding month of February 2010 and beyond, I learnt the value of keeping calm and having the faith that the SLT team, where it is a supportive one, will support you. Knowing what you value, as long as you believe, uphold and live your values, eventually, staff will come to respect you as they see what you hold true to yourself. It all boils down to the job at hand: taking care of our students, making a school world a better place.

What I know about everything I gained from the early days is that it was the right decision to progress up. It was hard. It was demanding but, slowly and gradually, I learnt to lead my way.

A year into my job and as part of my performance management conversation, I was asked if I would be interested in studying for the NPQH: the National Professional Qualification for Headship. There was no way I was ready for this. I still had two toddlers and was feeling very guilty about the amount of time and effort I was giving to this job that I couldn't match when I got home for the sheer exhaustion. I said no.

The following year, I was asked again, this time with more conviction that it was necessary for succession planning and that, in me, they could see the potential. I politely declined again and asked them not to ask me again but said I would say when I was ready. There is something about being a woman and then being Black that makes you hesitate. The self-talk can be defeatist and convinces you that there is still a way to go.

If I am honest, there is this niggle that rumbles in your mind all the time. It tells you that your heritage and the challenges have hindered your abilities. That you are not ready and you will make a fool of yourself and you don't want to do that! It forges a 'try harder' principle and a 'master it' philosophy that means you never believe you are there. So, you carry on working harder. By the time you turn around, you notice that a couple of other colleagues, counterparts who are probably male, Caucasian, or both, have moved on, progressed upwards with no hesitation at all. It didn't bother me, as I firmly felt I had some more growing up in leadership to do.

Little did I know that this complex is a perpetual theme amongst Black women concerning progression at work. A blog article on the WomenEd website (WomenEd is an organisation that focuses on the representation of women in leadership roles in education, with a specific focus on women with ethnic heritage), entitled *'Gender and middle leadership: A personal reflection'*, quotes some research which found that a study by sociologist Natasha Quadlin (2018) sought to investigate how gender and academic performance impact employment outcomes for recent college graduates. Quadlin found that men with high Grade Point Averages were twice as likely to get a call back than women candidates, based on their CV or résumé. Quadlin puts this down to gender stereotyping.

In her article, she states,

> Employers value competence and commitment among men applicants, but instead privilege women applicants who are perceived as likeable. This standard helps

moderate-achieving women, who are often described as sociable and outgoing, but hurts high-achieving women, whose personalities are viewed with more scepticism.

Given that I was no wallflower, nor a mousy type, my deep throaty voice from my short five-foot-four-inch body seasoned with a hint of enough attitude to command attention, could mean I fell in the second group, the high-achieving ones viewed with scepticism. A little bit damned if you do and damned if you don't.

Exuding assertiveness does not always bode well for women and, in the back of the mind of the Black woman, you know you always run the risk of being called the 'aggressive Black woman', with its connotations of being a 'right bitch', instead of the one who is just mission-focused. Nevertheless, in the line of duty of senior leadership, where you are placed to do what others can't or won't, you just cannot afford to be anything else, especially in schools.

The fact that I reiterated repeatedly to myself that I was less than ready is a concept familiar to many in the corporate world. In an article in the *Harvard Business Review*, 'Why Men Still Get More Promotions than Women' (Ibarra et al., 2010), they talk about women most likely needing what they call 'sponsorship'; I call it 'championing'.

In this article, they see the options of sponsorship waning the higher a female progresses in her career and, just when she needs it most, sponsorship is not there.

Women are viewed as 'risky' appointments for the CEO roles, especially from within their firms. Where women were hired, they tended to be from outside. This does somehow make my experience of going for the deputy head role tally with this notion. I will talk about that in the next chapter. Remember I was asked to do the National Professional Qualification for Headship in my year 2 of senior leadership? Well, I did complete the NPQH, but it took me 4 years to eventually embark on it.

11. The Journey to Headship

'Smooth seas do not make skilled sailors.'
[African proverb]

In Brené Brown's book *Dare to Lead* (Brown, 2018) she talks about shame and rumbling with vulnerability. It is the shame that we often try to mask and try to hide. I've been guilty of doing this several times and I have to admit I have become quite good at it too. Have you ever had to do the walk of shame?

The walk of shame after you have been rejected from a job in the same institution in which you work. It's a horrible feeling. The anguish, the stomach-churning, the butterflies, the sweaty palms, fear of the unknown when walking back into work amidst all your colleagues and students, who have been made aware or have been on the panel for the job that you've interviewed for.

This was me three times over at my school. It was not a nice feeling at all and yet I have come out of it unscathed. Well, I say unscathed, but this has been on the back of also dealing with a tremendous amount of imposter syndrome, anxiety and self-doubt.

Between the years 2014 and 2019, all I could do was keep thinking about ways that I could prove that I was worthy of my role. There were some experiences, some words and phrases, some actions, that required me to dig deep, very deep and soul search. I realise and recognise that all the experiences I've talked about so far in this book have helped to shape me to be the person I wanted to be and to become the courageous individual I envisaged myself embodying each day, and to fulfil my purpose.

Ofsted 2014

In May 2014, a school inspection team came in, bulldozed everyone, and made staff feel like they were doing a rubbish job. Our school had been surviving on the previously well-deserved 'outstanding' grade from Ofsted, the Office for Standards in Education, the UK's mega accountability and control body for educational services. In May 2013 the sound of an almighty thud could be heard, and the tremors felt so far when the school experienced an almighty fall from grace in the education world. It went from an 'outstanding' to a 'requires improvement' grade. In other words, from grade 1, we jumped two grades downwards to grade 3. We managed to scrape enough evidence to avoid the grade 4 – 'inadequate' – but it was very much touch and go.

Ouch, that hurt. I wasn't the head. I wasn't even the deputy head yet, but I was about to be. The school needed me and they didn't even know it.

I knew what the school needed and that was a deputy headteacher in charge of teaching and learning. Someone with the gravitas, knowledge, expertise and credibility mixed with the passion to lead the whole school successfully in the area where I felt it was falling short. Because I had planted the idea of this, I somehow felt responsible.

It was down to me that there was a leader in charge of teaching and learning in the first place up until this point.

Up until 2014, there had been no single senior leader in charge of the core business of teaching and learning. How could that be? I found it a great omission that we had no leader for teaching and learning, the pedagogy and practice, the heart and soul, the bread and butter of the school. I was an assistant headteacher for staff development and performance, my passion was teaching and learning and I had convinced the headteacher to allow me to carve out my niche in this area under my title. It was working, but it was very much in its infancy. Add to that the unusual line management tactics of my immediate line manager, the kind that liked to delegate plenty and then take all the credit, resulting in a very inconsistent approach to the leadership of teaching and learning.

Most of the time, I found myself buzzing with ideas, innovation and creation and blurting it all out in those meetings. Days later, those ideas were to be concocted into a mixture of embellished proposals and disingenuous intentions. My line manager was unable to convey them as compellingly as I did though, as the ideas were mine. There is only one version of me and therefore one version of the original.

This scene was a regular occurrence and each time it made me cringe at the big round table. Yet who was I to say anything? I just let it happen. I would become very frustrated but kept my cool. Two middle-aged white males, who were my superiors, having discussions about a presentation which I knew to be unnatural and definitely not heartfelt because it centred on my original ideas, were not to be interrupted, certainly not by me. Each time I did, there was an unusual stare from both parties. I wasn't ever quite sure what they were saying and if the disdain on their faces was directed at me or each other.

All I know is it felt awkward and uncomfortable. I am glad to say that I have learnt to become comfortable being uncomfortable. That is growth right there. Back then, these shenanigans continued until I could take it no more. Just at the point when I was going to ask for changes, they came. Before long, my line manager had been moved on and they needed a new deputy headteacher.

Seven years in and after watching the carry-on and the mess that was still somehow called 'leadership' unfold, I finally felt ready. It was my time to upgrade. There could not have been a better time to shine. We knew we were due to have an Ofsted inspection and I believed the focus of this would give me the drive to rise to the challenge of being a deputy headteacher.

DEPUTY HEAD APPLICATION 1

Teaching is my vocation. It's my passion, it's my love. For the first interview round, I was up against five white males. It was a gruelling experience. In all honesty, I went into it then, even though I did prepare, as best I could, doing my research with the greatest diligence. Preparing for leadership roles takes it out of you, but that is only the beginning. The amount of effort and energy you have to put in, whilst at the same time juggling your current role, is immense and intense. It leaves you drained and exhausted and, at the end of it, you hope that you have invested well and that you will exit the vanquisher, come out with the prize – in other words, that you've successfully been appointed. In the first round, I wasn't appointed. I half knew by the time I got to the feedback stage that I wouldn't be appointed. I then decided to go for the job again – call me a mug, but actually in reality this is what I needed to do.

Round 1 DH application and interview process

> 10 May 2013
>
> *Well, it is two days after the whole ordeal ended. From Tuesday 7 to Wednesday 8 May I was involved with the interview process as a candidate. What an ordeal! It really was gruelling but very interesting and has made me see exactly how to prepare. Put it this way, those 'Leader' magazines that I am bombarded with monthly from ASCL will now form part of my daily or at least weekly reading and my eyes are open so I will digest the information in them a little differently now.*
>
> *Firstly there was the issue of being an internal candidate. Out of thirteen applicants, six of us were shortlisted. By the time we had started Day 1, half way through, one had pulled out*

which left five. It involved meeting with and observing colleagues teach.

After a 'goldfish bowl' exercise, one of the candidates immediately set onto me, asking me a direct question about data, etc. At first I was a little put off, then I realised what she was trying to do, so calmly said: 'Are you asking me directly for information about the school?' She said yes and turned to the others, as if to get their support. I simply replied, 'Well, I think that's a question for when you get to the interview panel perhaps. Shall we get to prioritising, as we are on a time limit?' Silly woman, she had 10-inch heels and eyelashes from here to Euston ... I couldn't see the headteacher working with her.

She wasn't selected to return the next day.

I was. I couldn't help wondering if that was only because I was an internal candidate and the panellists felt obliged to do so.

We also had to answer questions from a 15-strong student panel! Again, I knew most of them.

We had a hefty data exercise to complete where we had to look at a Panda (old term for a report that tells you how well a school is performing) and write about 'What would be the main issues to bring to the SLT meeting?' and 'What would be the suggested strategies to take forward?' I was told later that this was the same exercise given to aspiring heads at the headteacher interviews!!!

Finally, we had to socialise / meet with the SLT. The challenge throughout the day was to remain focused and to also not feel perturbed by being the internal candidate. I also felt conscious that knowing everyone would make the candidates feel it was biased, so I tried to remain objective and not be too close to my peers but it was difficult. In some ways, it's easier to be an outsider as you have no association.

Day 2 we had to deliver an assembly about 'Interdependence' and then another panel interview which lasted 1 hour and 20 minutes. I have to say this was the most challenging part of the whole process and I realised about half way through that I was not answering as confidently as I would have liked to. I was floundering. It also opened up the lack of knowledge I feel in certain areas.

Outcome: unsuccessful.

The staff at my school were so supportive, many thinking I had actually been successful in applying for the post. I dreaded coming back the next day, but in fact it was fine. And even the two Year 9s from the student panel didn't ask me about the outcome! That was unusual, I thought.

Oh well, question is ... will I try again if it is advertised? Am I ready? I sure am ready to do the NQPH though and to see how I can gain more experience. Very scary all this, but extremely exciting!

I felt slightly embarrassed and would feel better with immediate feedback. Although I was told not to worry and that they are well aware of how much I contributed to the school.

The activities and reflections for this role were as follows:

Data exercise: did okay

Student Panel: apparently, the best received

Peer observation: my judgements were on point

Assembly: went well

Interview: I didn't mention the word 'deputising'

Allegation question: I didn't say 'I would speak to the head'. I need to also know about LADO if and when needed – well, what on earth?

I just think I didn't prepare well enough for this.

Highlights that my teaching and learning area is no doubt good but other areas I am not involved in as much.

Financial challenges -

Well, making sure what you cut is furthest away from cuts to the classroom as much as possible is the number one answer!

But now I am armed with feedback and what and how much to prepare for the next round, I just need to do this. It has definitely made me see the mileage but also that it is achievable to me. I need to continuously work on this. So I requested when I could begin the NPQH and he said, yes, asap, September, so I will research the info and put in my application!

I finally plucked up the courage to undertake the NPQH – five years after it was initially proposed to me. I got to a point where I needed to develop myself further. I had participated in numerous courses but I needed something to validate my work. In some ways, the lack of support and encouragement did me right, as I sought it by engaging in a high-level accreditation course. It is helpful when out networking and meeting others to do some research, and ask searching questions of any programmes you intend to take on. You then get a feel for what you will be putting yourself into.

In October 2013, my application to study for the NPQH with the National College was passed. I was deemed 'ready' to progress. That was it. I had taken the plunge myself, with no recommendation or impetus from another and proved to myself that, now, I was at least ready to study for it.

We were told we had 18 months from the start of our projects (so December 2013 in my case) to complete it. Even though I succeeded in applying, I had those nervous feelings again in my stomach, taking on a new venture. As a parent, you are always open to any type of life intrusions and these can affect your perspectives.

In January 2014, when everyone makes New Year resolutions, I had recorded the following:

1-New year, new ideas, new challenges, new opportunities

January 2014

So I have just spent quite a bit of time deciding upon which 'note-taking' app I should use from now on to log my journal entries. So much on offer! Time-consuming just to decide this, too much choice is the problem. After flitting back and forth between OneNote and Evernote, the latter I have been using for much longer, I have finally decided to use OneNote. I love the interface and the section capacity.

Anyway, I am embarking on the NPQH course and after what seems like a challenging first week back at work, not to mention challenging first week of the year, I feel I need to keep a track of my thoughts as time goes along.

'I want to see your mum, I wish I saw her, I never got to see her on Earth ... At least I will see her when I get to Sky' – this was the statement made by my 9-year-and-1-day-old first-born in the car as I drove us to the A&E department. My heart beat fast ... Was this a sign? Is this a sign? As the issue is still there. It seems I have been hoping that nothing will come along and discombobulate me from this course. I have placed it on such a high echelon, knowing that I am aiming for the very top, to become a headteacher, after what must be 10 years of convincing myself that possibly I have a chance at getting

there. My fear of anything inhibiting me from studying hard, well and performing my best, has already begun to become a reality ... Or so I think, as on Friday I noticed my son had a little bump in the middle of his neck. I took him to the GP and he recommended an ultrasound scan. However, what I forgot to do was ask: 'And how long do you think it will be before we get the appointment and for the actual scan to happen?'

So there I was, after coming home on his birthday, and sitting next to him, observing him, I see his right collar bone protruding a little further than the other. This sends me into utter panic.

I didn't eat much or sleep at all that day, only Tuesday of the first week back, and I was absolutely shattered. Not to mention, I freaked out, so much so I was just elated to know I still had the very large pack of 'Calms' in the cupboard. I had to take two and went to try to sleep eventually, after thinking all sorts about what this may be and then panicking and crying. My body was actually trembling. As I went into the bedroom, an advert came up about the big C and in my mind the question: 'Is this a sign?' I kept asking hubby, 'Am I overreacting?' to which he simply replied, 'No, you're just being a mum.' Wasn't sure where to place that, in the 'I'm normal and okay compartment' or in the 'He's just saying that to make me feel normal' or 'He doesn't know quite what to say' camp.

Wednesday was horrible and in my mind also the thoughts of how one keeps their cool, manages all that is happening on the work front while there is utter mayhem going on internally in one's mind. It felt as though I was being prepared and thrown in at the deep end. I mean, how I will cope if anything goes on during my course? It seems to mean so much to me. I don't want to fail or find myself facing difficulties as it will only contribute to my feeling of being a Black female, sort of at the top, but surrounded by white male counterparts, sometimes who make me, unwittingly to them of course, feel inadequate or that they don't expect me to be up to much – even though I have proven myself several times.

I just think that this is the pattern of thought that us people of colour have, as we always have to prove ourselves, over and over again.

Wednesday evening ... I took him to A&E. I cried. Doc said she would be the same way. Not sure if this was just 'doctor speak' to make me not feel so ridiculous or genuine. Anyway, I decided to take it as genuine.

Came home, prayed, asked my hubby to pray, and he did ... Beautifully. I read Psalm 27 over and over again. Why should I be afraid, why?

So, shattered, sleepy and very concerned, I retired to bed.

By Friday, my frantic state had calmed down. I am now able to function again. X-ray and blood test was recommended and I feel a bit listened to, so it has helped.

So much so that I am now about to begin the reading which I couldn't even attempt.

If there is anything that is going to be a challenge, it is making sure my children are safe, healthy and well.

Bring on the reading ... And let me tell you, about 100 pages in only 2 weeks! Let's see how it goes ...

Ciao for now ...

You can see from the summary of my week above that this period of time was dominated by personal events. Many of us as leaders will be behind masks as we continue to carry out our roles effectively at work. As a deputy head in school, you are caught between the rest of the SLT and the headteacher. Without any peers you can release the mask in front of, it can be a very lonely place. It is always worthwhile seeking the friendship of some who are peers within your organisation as well as outside of it.

The NPQH course was going to be the route to headship. I had not desired to be a headteacher in two years but I was going to run with their rhetoric anyway. I was really excited after reading through the handbook and even more so when I discovered I would be working with a coach. The benefits of courses that make us self-reflect are that they get deep inside our persona and make us find answers to the questions about ourselves we hold within. I would advise all leaders to ensure they continually develop themselves professionally. A good leader always has a sense of self-awareness. Feeling out of your depth is usually a sign that you are growing.

2-Am I ready? Out of comfort zone

January 2014

This week I experienced two clear situations where I felt totally out of my comfort zone. One was sitting in the SLT meeting next to our new but current HT nevertheless, and having to read and discuss our analysis in pairs of what we deduced from the Raise online data document. Although I like data and like talking to it, I found it a challenge due to the openness of it all and still I felt a lack of confidence about it.

Secondly came the governors' meeting at my sons' primary school for which I didn't feel too prepared and felt I should have been able to contribute more. Especially in my capacity as a senior leader in a school, I should have been able to share my understanding of progress at KS2 and what is expected.

Thirdly, discussions about the new school and the curriculum organisation seemed to go over my head. They always do.

Anything to do with timetable and looking at the whole school make-up of hours, staff, etc. I don't particularly like this sort of thing.

And finally, the information I found out about headteachers needing to have the very difficult conversations about redundancies with colleagues – 'It's enough to put you off' she said, but I reframed, 'Yes, true, but you do what has to be done.'

Well, at least I have some resources to help me, so I need to swot up.

If or when Ofsted come, I want to feel I know my stuff!

It highlighted to me, in my reframing, that these are just areas I need to work on and work towards to gain more confidence in … Oh, where is that affirmation book from Tony Swainston again …?

Having a couple of affirmations, mantras, that are positive and that help you get mind over matter, can be very helpful. *The 7 Cs of Leadership Success* (Swainston T, 2012) is a good book to refer to if you are not able or not in the mode of thinking up positive affirmation statements.

THE NPQH

The NPQH application on its own was demanding but, given the role it is preparing you for, so it ought to be. The course representatives spoke of a condition of the course being achieving headship in two years. The entire process gave me the courage, but I was going slowly – the courage to go for the deputy head role a second time.

Deputy Head application ... here we go again, round 2

5 Feb 2014

I feel scared, nervous and anxious. Not enough time, lots to do, am I up for this, why don't I believe in me as much as others do or is it me being 'humble', not bigging myself up?

Well, I must have some self-belief as I am applying. I have already begun filling in the form which in itself is daunting but added to that fact it's already Wednesday, 20:39. Thursday is options evening so a late day for me with a full day's work; Friday too, a full day with the boys going to taekwondo in the evening which leaves really the night times and Saturday for me to get this done before Monday ...

That is why I am anxious. I recently also made two mishaps that the head called me in to discuss: the time I didn't meet with the Swedish teachers and, instead, prioritised my meeting with the external colleague. I had gone ahead, ignoring my head's request and invited Ali in to meet me, in spite of the request, and can you believe, today I missed my 'on call'. I was at the wrong site entirely!!! What DH-in-the-making makes this kind of error??? And just before APPLICATION TIME ...

Wow, no pressure then. Deep breathing, prayer ... and off I go ...

I was the only female amongst the candidates. But at least this time there was one representation from somebody who was not white. An Asian man, although I took one look at him and thought, whilst I'm in a school that's predominantly Asian in population, this guy doesn't stand a chance against me. I had on my lucky silvery-grey suit with the pencil skirt. I felt the part. I held my head up high, wore the hell out of that skirt suit as best

I could and strutted around the school as one of the candidates in this interview group on tour.

I smiled at my peers as they winked, nodded or secretly held a thumbs up as they passed me by, huddled with the group. I had chosen to do it this time just in case my apparent absence was a considered factor in the previous interviews. Yet again I was put through the gruelling process of having to answer the multitude of questions prepared in a different way with a slightly different style. You get a sense that if you fail in your own school then, perhaps, you're not good enough because that's where you should be excelling and at your best. I was never somebody who became complacent about going for a job in a school. I never would be, yet it was challenging.

I put my heart and soul into the interview process. To make matters worse, everyone was waging on me, everyone from the cleaner to other members of the leadership team and of course several students now knew and, for their own special reasons, believed that I was the right candidate and that I would be a success on this round, having been open and honest about it. This was especially as some of my own students that I taught were a part of the interview panel on the first round. A sureness had grown amongst the student population that I would definitely succeed in becoming the deputy head this second time. I nailed the teaching and learning panel, the data task, the lesson feedback and the student panel.

Being the second time around, there was not a single one of the 50 questions for 'deputy head interviews' that I had not practised. There was nowhere I would allow for negative feedback. I was on my game. Things were looking very promising. It was between two Asian men, one other internal white male and another external white male candidate and me. I was not called back for Day 2.

DH interview process 2 – the aftermath, Feb 2014

16 Feb 2014

So it never happened. Well, I did apply, and I did get shortlisted, and I did conduct interview Day 1. However, they decided not to bring anyone back for Day 2!

My husband was wicked in helping me to cut it down, provide insights and my friend provided his attention to gist and detail ... I was shortlisted. Not that I doubted I would be.

There were seven applicants, or at least shortlisted on the paper, but in the morning only five were present.

Once again, there was a series of activities and an interview panel which included the following questions:

From what I can remember the questions went like this:

1. What are the strengths of the school and the areas for development or weaker areas?

2. What is your idea of 'leadership'?

3. You know our vision but is there anything that you think is missing or that you would want to see in there that is not mentioned?

4. What does the school mission statement mean to you?

5. What are your values?

6. Can you give an example of how you have had financial management of a budget and what impact you had?

7. 4 HR scenarios:

a. How would you deal with a member of staff you manage who is repeatedly off sick?

b. A student comes to tell you his teacher has banged his head against the wall – what do you do?

... and two more which I don't remember.

9. Describe yourself in one word.

That was followed by the data task and, interestingly, after being at a curriculum governor committee meeting only the night before till 9:10 p.m. with heated discussion about the data and the strategies for the pupil premium and the achievement of Black students – mainly 'BCRB' which is the DfE's ethnicity code for Black Caribbean. This conversation has been happening countless times in several governing bodies for aeons and it just does not seem to ever go away.

The task involved reading a Raise online data report for an anonymised school and answering three questions:

1. What are the issues for attainment?

2. What are the issues for achievement?

3. What strategies would you put in place?

We got our envelopes and were told that we would be called to be told what would happen the next day.

Another assembly on what 'Community means' and an interview with a full panel followed.

That evening I went to my friend's house and we were discussing the experience. My heart was in my mouth as I attempted to put on a brave face and be upbeat and optimistic about it all.

As it happens, my attempts were squashed when I received the call and was told that they weren't calling anyone back for the second day of interviews as they felt there was not a big enough field, and that tomorrow I would be told what that meant 'personally' for me.

So back I went again. The next morning, I got dressed, put on my favourite outfit, paid attention to my hair. making sure I looked bright and perky and took my beat-up ego back to school.

However, this time as I walked in, surprisingly, I felt no nervousness, shame or rejection. I knew I was a strong candidate and asked the headteacher to squeeze in a time during the day to give me a brief breakdown of what it meant 'personally' to me.

Here it goes: I was told I was the strongest of the candidates, in fact, way ahead and the governors thought it would not be worth bringing anyone else back for Day 2, so they did not go ahead! Err, if that's so, then why not just make me go through the second day and employ me? I didn't ask this though but, after speaking with many, who were as surprised and confused as I was by the decision, I considered doing research into the equality of opportunity clauses in appointments of senior leaders.

I felt a little injustice but not too much to be angry or upset or anything. I thanked panel members and my seniors for the opportunities afforded to me, for allowing me to do the NPQH and the career development programme. I asked if they thought I should apply again, to which they responded 'definitely'. However, I was not 100% sure that I would want to.

Although it wasn't to be and I was called into the small room once again and told I had not been successful, my mindset had somewhat shifted. On this occasion, when I asked why I hadn't been successful, I felt in a much stronger position than before. I was told they wanted to go out again or rethink the position. Be that as it may, I knew what the real reason was, or at least what I sensed was the real reason, and I could see no other rationale for why I would not be appointed to the job except that, as a Black woman, I represented something different to what they wanted.

My mind did that complex thing of being two-faced and sadly my self-esteem took a knock and I was catapulted to the 'not ready yet' days. The use of the word 'yet' is a growth mindset term. Growth mindset: a philosophy championed by names such as Professor Carol Dweck and Professor John Hattie. Those with growth mindsets have their cups always half-full and not half-empty.

The people I like to call 'reframers' are solution-focused and they problem-solve. They recognise that mistakes happen and learning is a natural process that they can unlock and learn from more and more. In teaching, when giving feedback, the use of the term 'yet' encourages young minds to have a growth mindset as it signals to a student that there is always the chance of getting there, it's not out of reach, you just haven't made it to the goal at this time. Using this demonstrates that somewhere in me I believed I would get there. I just needed to believe it. Still, not getting it 'yet' did nothing for the story I was writing in my head. It was that I represented a risk. A chance no one at the very least wanted to take in me. A risk that, unfortunately, I posed over and over again in the coming years as I sought my headship.

Nevertheless, I couldn't deny what had been affirmed. I meditated and visualised. For me, it worked. I was surrounded by well-wishers and had a wonderful and amazing coach in my husband I thought that I would be a deputy headteacher but perhaps not at this school and I became fine with that. I decided that I would persevere with what I needed to do if the opportunity arose elsewhere, which was:

- Focus on completing my NPQH to the best of my ability
- Learn all I needed to know
- Be certain about what my values were
- Create a mission statement for myself
- Regularly practise responses to those deputy head questions.

Failure was not an option. I had come this far. I would do it!

Know your worth

12. Deputy Headship

'The whole purpose of it is it's quite a self-directed desire to improve your practice ... there should be you as a professional continually looking at your own practice and saying, "How can I slightly alter what I'm doing to make my practice more effective?"'

They decided to interview again and, somehow, I found the courage in me to go for it a third time. It was hard. It was challenging, but I felt much more convicted and relaxed and wondered what more I could have learned, rehearsed and practised in preparation for this. I was ready. This week will definitely prove if I am due to be a deputy headteacher or not and whether all the work I had done previously, up until this point, had been worth it. However, all the work that I had done had prepared me and given me the skills for a time such as this.

Perhaps on this occasion it was because I knew that many of the school community were behind me on the second round that I felt much more at ease and confident. After all, I've been for it once before. I didn't even consider how it might feel walking back into school. I just had to hold up my shoulders and think, 'Well, if it's not meant to be here, it's meant to be somewhere else.'

On the third occasion I was also up against an internal candidate who was unsuccessful; it was advertised as a substantive post of permanent deputy headship and it was due to begin in September 2014. The interview lasted a gruelling hour and a half. You wouldn't believe that I had already been interviewed for this twice beforehand. Many had questioned and wondered why I hadn't been given the post first or even the second time, but there I was again.

Third time lucky – and the new 'interim' Deputy Head is ...

7 Apr 2014

Yes, you've guessed it … it's me! Appointed on Friday 28 March, after a gruelling almost 2 hours' interview with a panel of 4.

By the time I was given the announcement that I was going to be offered the job, I wasn't even elated. I just felt like saying, 'Well, thank you – I should think so too.'

Disappointingly, two days later, to my surprise when I opened my letter, looking forward to the contents, I looked at the top of the letter. In bold was written: 'Interim deputy headteacher'.

Interim? What the hell!? Who in their right mind would want to put me through my paces in such a way and then decide at the flick of a switch and at the drop of ink on the paper that this role would suddenly be transferred into an interim role? When I received the letter informing me of my success, it had in bold the word 'Interim' at the top. It turns out I was given the post for a year, subject to regular reviews.

I know that now that would not be allowed and thankfully the case is made that, for equality of opportunity, if you apply for a position and it is advertised as a substantive position, then that is what you should get.

They had changed my position from a substantive post to an interim one and I had not even had a conversation or a 'congratulations' yet.

I felt a total anti-climax. I was disillusioned, almost as if I was not deemed a real deputy head yet, and I guess I had to reframe as it was an opening. It was an opportunity, as they want me for the post but they see areas that need refinement.

Many would not have had these thoughts. What was it about myself that allowed me to make these justifications for others? I was playing back the questions they asked in the interview and wondering how I could have prepared myself even better. Even though I had been offered it, I still felt as though I could have prepared myself even better to deserve feeling high and a true sense of achievement. I thought achieving this would have created the same sense of accomplishment I had felt when I had succeeded in gaining other posts where I have felt 100% successful on my merit.

The knock-on effect of this could be detrimental for many aspirant leaders and some could be lost along the way. We could argue that perhaps they just do not have tenacity; however, there is only so much that individuals can and should take before they look away from an area where there is a much-needed workforce that represents those whom they serve.

The *TES* article 'Where are our BME leaders in education?' asks: 'With no BME leaders, how can we best tackle racism in our schools?' I am not sure this is the right question. Racism does not stem from schools but from the wider society, and the lid has been taken off the pot which has been closed for so long. We are now opened up to, and aware of, institutionalised racism and the inbuilt structural limitations of certain communities to become socially mobile. I do, however, agree with the general gist of this piece when it asks: 'With no BME leaders, how do we encourage BME students to aspire to be leaders themselves?'

The lack of representation from those who do not identify as white has been a realisation for many years. It is with a heavy heart that I look upon repeated articles, opinion pieces that discuss the disproportionate level of representation in leaders to the students in some schools, predominantly those in areas likely to be more diverse, of course. This article states that, due to the unconscious bias that exists, there will never be a chance to 'break the ceiling on career opportunities for BAME teachers'.

Unconscious bias seems to have become the new professional development session of the day. But it will take a lot for this to be eliminated, if it ever will be. I don't hold the answers. This book is about sharing a story so that others can find their ways to circumvent this issue and counter the statistics, one leader at a time.

I met with the headteacher and the chair of governors. I was informed that I would be reviewed every half-term to check how my progress had been with my targets and performance. Hell, no. It was not going to go that way. I made it very clear what my expectations of the role were and that the job had already been advertised as a substantive role and that is what it needed to be. I was not going to be subjected every half-term to some sort of interrogation and intense scrutiny of my performance, just to see if I measured up. Measured up to what?

After all, I had been appointed; clearly, I had what it took and this made me even more determined to prove myself. I was angry and exasperated that I kept needing to prove myself. Suddenly for the first time in my whole career, I asked: 'Is it because I am Black?'

What other explanation could there be? I had been on the turbulent journey with the school through three Ofsted inspections, one 'good', the second 'outstanding' and the third 'requires improvement', and I had shared my vision of moving forward, recognising the contributions of everyone including myself in the process.

During a conversation with my NPQH coach, I brought up the point about my position suddenly becoming 'interim'.

14 May 2014

Today I had the second out of six possible coaching sessions with my coach. It went well, I thought, and we covered a lot of ground, including my approach to the HT about the letter which states that my role will be reviewed termly, with termination, should the governors consider that the acting up arrangement should be! I wasn't pleased with the tone of the letter and after arranging a meeting with the HT (cancelled due to Ofsted!) but went ahead today, I felt much more reassured.

What was positive was that the head said this was not the intention of the letter and that HR had tried to find wording to suit the termly review. I objected to the 'termination' aspect and asked that the letter be re-written. He said he felt it would not come to that at all and that he was not 'setting me up to fail'. I was glad he said it and not I, as this is exactly what I was sensing and feeling and I let him know so. He reassured me this was not the case and that he already could sense the following year would be great for the school.

This really helped me to see that HTs are real and they understand.

I thought the meeting went well. My coach felt this meeting went well too.

I began to use Facebook to post picture affirmations of myself with my 'Self-Talk' and acts of positive engagement with students whenever things felt a little bogged down or rough or my 'mood' was not in the right place for the day. It's a strategy I use to this day. Children and young people have an incredible way of helping you get out of your pity-party. The strap line for each of my messages was 'Know your worth'. It became my mantra. I would reflect on the contributions I put into school improvement, daily, weekly, half-termly or just whenever I reminded myself to do so. It's the act of building oneself up, driving up your self-confidence.

I also came away from my coaching session with some action points to progress with my NPQH placement impact initiative, a contact to make, and another idea for my home school impact initiative, looking at what another school did for teaching and learning, and observations.

I remember when we went to the BME career development programme, the facilitator talked about how people never apply for jobs they are already good at or that they already know or do, and it's true and it's growth, but boy this was really uncomfortable and more so because it followed a roller-coaster of emotions. This was my third time. I had sat through a total of eight panels across the interviews. This final experience was the longest and most gruelling.

There were four members on the panel there and I was asked questions which deviated terribly from those that were on the sheet, but in fact they needed to be and they were helpful both for me and for them, I guess. Still, I think I should have looked at my 360 a bit more; the question I have for myself is how much swotting up could I and should I have done? I did lots of reading but I was stumped, I forgot to mention that the most important curriculum changes are the change to making examinations linear, to the point where I felt as though I was being helped by the school improvement partner, almost as though they knew I knew it but I wasn't able to articulate it. And this is my fear about not being able to articulate my ideas. I know that I achieve excellence in teaching and learning and driving teaching and learning and yet I found it hard to articulate exactly what I lead and drive on. I know that I have emotional intelligence but I didn't use the phrase 'educational excellence'. I did talk about elevation through education, how everyone can succeed, and drew on exemplars from the achievement for all programme but it's almost like I want to have my own phrasing and I want to have it my way so that people listen and go 'wow, yes', same things but said in a different way, in a more influential and spontaneous and charismatic way.

Yes, I kind of feel disheartened. I almost feel that I don't really deserve it; maybe it just needs to simmer and sink in. Even when I got the call, I had to say to myself, 'Miriam, sound animated', because I felt that I sounded monotone, and like this 'all right, thank you' rather than 'wow, excellent, thank you, that's great news! This is brilliant, I look forward to working with you, Phil' – you know, something like that. I didn't feel like saying that; I just took it on the chin. I think I was just drained.

And it makes me think about how far I am really from a headship and how much more I've got to learn and grow.

IMPACT!!!! Perseverance and conviction pay off ... letter re DH post

So after my brilliant coaching and liaising, result. I received an email stating that the 'interim and regular review' section will be removed from the letter, so I await the redrafted letter to confirm my position for the year.

My vision of work as a deputy headteacher differed from my experience in a few ways. I possibly had too romantic an idea of it, to be honest. It started off all wrong with my letter of appointment and led to two very emotionally tumultuous and traumatic years.

For the first two years of leading teaching and learning as a deputy head, I worked non-stop on the cause. The mission: destination 'outstanding'. Ofsted's high accountability structure means that those in leadership feel the weight of the work at hand and the judgement that will be made on this work. The school was good in all but one area, teaching and learning, and there was work to do and we had two years to do it in, before the inspectors would descend upon us once again and swarm the building, intruding on lessons and interrogating our every thread of strategic planning and evidence of the impact of our actions.

We had to do away with the complacency, we had to clean up the pedagogy and we had to train the students in our new philosophies so their hearts and minds were behind our drive.

This took a lot of time and plenty of professional dialogue. Some took place behind closed doors, delivering messages about the quality of teaching and learning not quite meeting the expectations, often with line managers present. It involved enduring backlashes from some who felt it was criticism, tears from those who felt like they were letting down the team or themselves and also those who were in the 'resistance' team. Stoic defenders of 'we have always done it this way'. It required a culture change and, as the saying goes, 'culture eats strategy for breakfast'. Without the right culture, any strategy I intended to put in place would be eaten up for breakfast without the buy-in of the majority.

In my mind, the response to the naysayers was 'Well, if we continue to do what we have always done, we will always get what we always got.' That kept me focused and determined to move us on. This was not a school delivering a satisfactory standard of education and I, like many of my colleagues, had worked too hard to be relegated to a satisfactory team member of a 'satisfactory' school, the grade 3 judgement from Ofsted. Things had to change.

Becoming a headteacher, I have a renewed appreciation of the pressure that was put upon me to deliver. As a head, your neck is on the line ultimately. It is you that represents the school, although it is important to recognise the value and the importance of the team you work with. The pressures at times did not make me feel as though I was doing the right thing and I found myself looking for approval for almost every action and decision I was making. Second-guessing yourself at every point is a sure way to destroy your character and self-belief. I would return home with questions and I would rumble over this with my husband.

Talking about this over dinner more than paying attention to our home life became the norm. This was until my dear husband put his foot down and banned me from talking about work. It needed working out, of course, but our home was not that place every day. He was right.

I worked with a great team of teachers and leaders but I specifically remember feeling very disheartened that one area I had sought approval from or direction had let me down. Stepping into deputy headship, line management felt different and to this day I wondered why. There had been a shift in the working relationship and I couldn't put my finger on it. Or, it could be argued, I refused to admit what it might be, putting it down always to just my perceptions.

Previous line management of me by a colleague I previously held in admiration for their high level of knowledge, skill and expertise, one who had been inspirational and forthcoming, had disintegrated into a battle of wills. I understand that being very proactive, a doer and a finisher, may have meant that I was seen to be the right person to deliver. However, it came across as pressurising, sometimes even near to bullying. I remained steadfast.

I lost sleep between the years 2014 and 2016 but I grew plenty during this time. Two intense years of making change. My NPQH coach had warned me too, quoting to me the statistic that 70% of change processes fail. But determined me decided that this statistic was something I would brush off, thinking: I'll strive to be in the 30% that don't.

Ofsted 2016

'We did it! Actually, Miriam did it.' That was the comment that came from one of the assistant heads, who I completely hold in high regard and respect for the quality of her work, so when a compliment comes from a peer like that, you take it on board and you smile, albeit sheepishly. This is because you missed the joy in the euphoria of being given the 'good' with many elements described as 'outstanding' in the area you lead. A joy that is quickly robbed from you as you notice that not everyone is showing agreement with your accolades.

Working alongside what was previously an excellent line manager; finding myself a minority at all the senior training sessions; being asked questions that would not have been asked of others; facing pushbacks every time I had ideas; sometimes being 'shushed' at the table; facing microaggressions – not quite knowing what they were but feeling them, was hard. Feeling the fear and doing things anyway, only to come across barriers. I denied it, I didn't want to believe it.

I was told about it, told what would happen in some circumstances, warned of jealousies, but I didn't and couldn't comprehend it nor see valid reasons for why that would be. Eventually, I surrendered. There had to be a greater force, and I know it was not the will of God, or divine interventions but interventions of a different kind, people power, people in power, in a profession I love so much. I was finally tasting the elixir of venom at the top. It was the only time in my career I asked if this was what racism in education felt like.

In May 2014, I wrote a frustrated entry entitled 'Last minute dot com!' Due to the nature of being given many tasks that needed urgent attention at a moment's notice. It felt as though someone was avoiding these jobs, but communication was not evident.

It followed a series of actions I found frustrating, and I would like to offer a few pointers for any headteachers out there who misinterpret the role of a deputy and the meaning of 'to deputise'.

A deputy headteacher has probably stepped into the role to fully back and support the work of the headteacher to fulfil their vision.

It is absolutely fine to request your deputy step in for you, but spare a thought for them and their workload. They too have a diary and a schedule of events they will be working their way through. All because they want to do their jobs well, of course.

Time is such a precious resource for everyone, not just the head. It shows great respect and yields many rewards and spontaneous efforts of others going above and beyond when communication is clear and direct, when intentions are stated, when the wishes of your deputy are seriously considered and not disregarded. Like other colleagues, working to their strengths and learning to know what makes them tick, sparks their passion and enthusiasm and will do wonders for progressing the organisation. Consulting and deciding things together can go a long way too, and rather than feeling as though you are not in control or being a good leader, it will ensure your deputy feels valued and will continue to be your 'right-hand man or woman'.

As a result, I kept up with my memoirs and vowed never to treat my senior leadership in ways that contradict what I have mentioned above.

Next Christmas, oops, half-term will be different ...

27 Oct 2015

I am shaking, trembling at the thought of going to a gym class. Being so unfit, I see myself as the poor, fat, unhealthy girl in the corner who has not remembered what it feels like to stretch a limb, much less what the inside of a real gym looks like.

Oh well, this, I guess, is what happens when our thoughts and mind become so consumed with work. The intention is always there, but the reality of making the time and committing to it is not. And alas, the poor eating, late nights, alcoholic 'save me' beverages, coffee 'wake me up' mornings, rush for deadlines and so on take their toll. I have never felt so unfit. I remember saying this before but this time it's worse. I suppose, from now on, each time will feel worse as I get more youthfully-challenged too!

Work ... yes, work. How about the week I have just had where the HT has publicly, in front of the SLT, made me feel like the target of his long-held frustrations, shaped like a bullet and directed straight at my gut? My gut, being the area of the school I lead, teaching and learning. The heart and soul of every school, the mechanics, the engine which needs constant updating, servicing and TLC, lest it lose its price to depreciation.

It turns out I had felt this way because an item that had not been previously discussed with me had appeared as an item on our SLT meeting agenda and I was unprepared. The fact other SLT members spoke about it afterwards illustrated how out of character it was for me and therefore they knew I was being dumped in it.

This feeling of being undervalued every morning for a year and a half took its toll. My advice would be to definitely not let things fester or go on too long. This is where courage is necessary. The courage to approach your line manager and find the right tone with which to deliver your prose.

In my case, my opening went something like this: 'We began the same time, you were always my line manager and I considered you a very good one, being able to guide, having done my role previously and then pushing just enough for me to learn and grow. However, something happened, something changed and I am not sure what it is … but speaking to me in a way that makes me feel devalued, not heard and dismissed, does not the makings of a confident and supportive DHT make – which is what I am committed to being as part of the most senior trio in the school …'

It can be cathartic to hold a courageous conversation. After all, busy senior leaders can do without expending extra time on mulling over bad feelings which may hinder their proactivity. With so much to do in so little time, I wondered how many other DHTs felt the same way and yet managed to be resilient and courageous enough to stand up to any tests of character and persevere. I always knew it would not be easy, but when you are in it, it can be tough.

In my diary entry I continued:

I do think that this is all God's way of preparing me for headship. How else can I become the world's most awesome headteacher without standing the tests of time … and people!

So how will next term be different?

1. I need to do what is urgent and manage my time and the expectation of what can be achieved in the given time scale by sticking to my plans.

2. I need to continue to delegate, build positive relationships so this is easier to do.

3. I need to get my fitness back on track. Not sure how but I must.

I have heard of stories where colleagues have reached a point of frustration with the styles of leadership they are enduring, that they decide to work to rule, meaning they decide that the efforts they put into their work are not paying dividends or being recognised; they therefore decide they won't 'kill themselves' any longer but do only that which is required to get a job done. Nothing more. No more going above and beyond. I believe this is an aspect of self-preservation. There are always times as leaders when we need individuals to go above and beyond and looking after them helps to bank this.

As an aspiring leader, as you work out what you need to do, remember self-preservation is a must. There is a Ghanaian proverb that says, 'Even the lion, the king of the forest, protects himself against flies.' The lion is the boldest of the jungle, but it still guards itself against something which seems minuscule but can still cause some harm or annoyance at the very least.

I can honestly say I had never worked so hard in my life as from 2014 to 2016. In her blog article advising leaders to take a break, Jill Berry mentions a conversation she had which mirrors some I have had with those outside of education. The question she says that her business manager asked was, 'Can you tell me whether this is normal? It seems that everyone here works themselves into the ground in term time. By the time the holidays arrive, they're in a state of near-collapse. They rest and recover during the break, but then the new term starts and it begins all over again. Is this just what teachers and leaders in schools do?' I am sure many would answer, reluctantly, 'yes', and then do a double-take and see how self-destructive this behaviour is. Leaders, please. Look after yourselves.

What we inevitably do is risk working too hard, exhausting ourselves in the process, rendering us no good to anyone.

If you have a supportive boss who believes in developing others, chances are you will be on the upward trend in levels of confidence.

When you have a boss or a leader who criticises your every move you are even more vulnerable and risk running out of any fight. You are left with two choices. One, start to believe them and mistrust your ability to perform your role; or two, trust yourself, your higher power and the fact that you are already in role with the achievement record you have so far, and blow your boss's perceptions up into smithereens.

You are reading this book now because I chose the latter. I reclaimed the power over my life. It wasn't easy but overpowering the chatter monkey in my head, all the noise he kept making, I had to just slap him down and shut him up, for good.

It took me four years but I did it.

13. Using My Superpowers

'You gain strength, courage and confidence by every experience in which you really stop to look fear in the face. You are able to say to yourself, "I lived through this horror. I can take the next thing that comes along." You must do the thing you think you cannot do.'

(Eleanor Roosevelt)

Eleven applications, eight interviews

At this point, I am shouting out one headteacher who congratulated me and said, 'At least you did it in less time than me.' Apparently, she got her headship at interview number 13. It just goes to show, the journey differs for everyone and it is not an indication of how good a headteacher you are in the making. This headteacher led the school to 'outstanding' in 2012 and went on to lead an international school successfully in another part of the world thereafter.

Application Number 1 – North Wynford

It could not have happened at a more opportune time. I was totally committed to leaving my current establishment and had decided I was no longer going to look for any more headteacher positions if I was unsuccessful, but I'd be damned if I would continue to stay where I had lost my sense of partnership-working and would not submit myself any longer to the ups and downs of 'worthiness' I was perpetually experiencing from one year or term to the next. I had a lot to give and the frustration was overwhelming me.

I remember when I was studying for the NPQH and someone in our group said, 'I suppose you know when you are ready for headship: when you look at the current head and feel you can do everything better.' Maybe not always better, I would say, but certainly differently.

In England's teacher recruitment cycle, the deadline for teacher resignations is 31 May if you want to leave your school. This in turn translates to that being the very last date that a school can make an appointment, supposedly. Hardly anyone resigns then though, as it always falls in the half-term week, so the final dates that teachers are usually appointed is just before the half-term begins, the final week of May into June. I was one of such teachers to get my appointment within that close proximity to the deadline.

On 24 May 2019, I achieved what I had set out to do. I had successfully been appointed as a headteacher.

When the chair of governors said those words to me, 'We would like to offer you the post', my eyes glazed over instantly. I hadn't thought about how I might need to compose myself should I be successful. How weird. I had always prepared for disappointment, and thought about what I might think and talk about doing in those first 90 days. But never had I considered the immediate seconds following the appointment. I was over the moon and suddenly felt the urge to use the 'little girls' room'. Somehow, I managed not to scream aloud. I simply showed as best I could how elated I was, and graciously thanked my panel for the opportunity and for making my day.

With poise, elegance and being cool, calm and collected, I stood up and walked out of the door. Err, no, not exactly! In fact, I was so happy, I jumped up out of my chair and did a mini clap. Realising I was really, really ecstatic, I did express my gratitude for the opportunity, my eyes did glaze over and I did prevent myself from crying, I did show how happy I was and, as the chair of governors spoke to me, I thought of how excited I would be going home and informing my husband.

Then it happened – that embarrassing moment that I will never be able to take back, as I was bidding farewell to the panel members; I spoke last with the chair of governors and then I hugged her! Just like that, it was spontaneous. But it felt natural. It was only as I walked down the stairs, I thought: 'Miriam, you fool, why did you do that? How could you hug the chair of governors, you twat? – you probably looked like a little kid, not a headteacher.'

Months later, I raised it with her. She did not bat an eyelid. It was so natural and that's when I knew, as one of my guardian angels had said to me, 'You will know when you have your school – they will want you as much as you want them.' He was right. But the journey to get to this point was not easy.

I knew it would be a long shot, but as I have said to myself countless times, 'If you don't try, you will never know' and think of how you will feel telling your grandchildren, 'Oh, I wish I had.' Inevitably, there will be moments when we will have wished, but essentially, while we have our physical abilities and our faculties, isn't life about making the most of every opportunity and having no (or minimal) regrets?

With that in mind, I began, tentatively, to scour the *TES* newspaper that sat in the school staff room. It had been several years since I had picked up a copy of this bumper periodical packed with everything you need to know in the education world, including the all-famous jobs section. I had also wanted this to be done secretly; I didn't want to rouse suspicion and awkward questions about why I was looking in the *TES*, followed by potential rumours I may be leaving falling into the wrong ears.

Potentially, this could happen by being caught by the 'okra mouth', as my dad would say, the one who just cannot hold onto any information because their mouth is so slippery, like okras — some call them 'ladies' fingers'.

I would walk into the staffroom as if to go straight to my pigeon hole. Each time, as I strode across the staffroom, I would give a quick once-over at the main room and the annexe, covered with individuals' belongings, coats, bags, student books, marking pens, board pens, walls covered in union posters, notifications of the day, cover notices, pictures from staff do's or trips and then, in the centre, the focal point, the middle of the room, the small coffee table – behold, there lay the copy of this week's *TES*. Some days it had been pulled apart by those considering their next moves, the magazine in one place and the paper parts in another.

Other days it looked untouched. With a final check to see if anyone lurked in the annexe or looked as though they might be leaving soon and catch me looking, I would quickly sit in the middle circle and jump right to the back where the adverts were, to see if there were any appropriate jobs for the role of headteacher. I did this over several months.

When I applied for the first headteacher job, I definitely was not ready. It was for a school being built which was a sister school to an already very successful one. It was going to be a brand-new building and brand-new school. Incidentally, this school never took off but that did not stop the award-winning and MBE CEO of the main school from pursuing and succeeding in establishing two further schools, and inheriting a third when the headteacher went AWOL. All this in the time it took me to get my first headship.

I know this as I had applied to two of the three schools. This first school would be a fresh start-up. I didn't even know what I needed to consider for a start-up school. I was dipping my toes into the water. It was low-risk and I had nothing to lose. I just wanted to gauge how close to headship I actually was. If I discovered there was a huge gaping gulf between where I was performing at the time and where I needed to be, I would quickly find out and relegate my efforts to a time in the future, maybe after polishing up my act a bit, swotting up a little more, learning extra things and then going for it again. But there was no hurry.

My strength, courage and confidence had developed but my superpowers of endurance and determination were really put to the test.

I was advised to ring to find out more about the school and I spoke with the executive headteacher herself. She said she looked forward to receiving my application. When I didn't get shortlisted, I was bolshie enough to call and ask if someone could give me feedback on my application. What made me think I could do that? I don't know but, to my surprise,I was told that the headteacher, one with an OBE I might add, was hoping I would call as she would happily give me feedback on my application. I guess she saw my potential. That is exactly what she said when I rang and, with her 'blessing', off I went feeling a sense of 'Yes, I am worthy of getting a headship and I can do this.'

I applied next to a local secondary school and I was acknowledged and invited to visit the school. 'That was quick,' I thought. I could potentially achieve getting the position after only two application rounds. Boy, was I wrong. I wasn't even shortlisted. At this stage, it didn't matter. Nor did it affect me. I had kept this to myself. The only people who knew I had applied for jobs were the headteacher and the personal assistant.

My husband was also in the 'knowing that Miriam has gone for an interview' club. I had requested that a song and dance was not made of this as I was just testing the water. It felt fine not to be shortlisted. I had not exposed myself to the potential of embarrassment and shame of not being successful. At this stage, it was still pretty much a private activity. Getting an acknowledgement gave me hope. It once again sent me a message that I had something there. There was clearly headship material evident somewhere amongst my skills and experience, even if I didn't truly believe it myself yet. I was told this by the executive headteacher.

I continued to look at the *TES* now and again and, in between these applications, I had to contend with some interesting experiences. First, there was the uncomfortable experience of telling my headteacher that I was looking for another job; and then there was anticipating how that individual would respond. Then there was contending with the changes in behaviours from the headteacher following my attendance at an interview. I remember returning and absolutely nothing was said to, or asked of, me. No questions, no comments, nothing. I was just being blanked.

When I saw the job package for another brand-new school opening up, I thought it was a sign. Remember earlier in the book I explained that my dad had always told me to 'be bold'. Let's just say the title of the school spoke to me. That should help to explain. I thought it was a given, I was destined to be there. I had applied when I was dipping my toes in the water but there was no shortlisting then. It was a non-entity. The funny thing was, I don't think the organisation themselves were ready and it seemed to be true as, a year later, here I was looking at a revamped packaging of the said new school.

I was told by a family friend that a new school was in the offing and that I should look out for the information and get in early, show an interest and be all over it. At this point, I was loosening the grip on shame and had let it slip to a few I was looking. It was okay – they acted as scouts!

Once again, I set about doing research, staying up at night, trawling the internet to cover anything I could find out about the school, the local community, any history, linked personalities, potential governors, primary schools and their performance, local media coverage both of the school and of anything to do with the community and so on.

This time, I could sense that this job meant a little more to me. It was more than putting my toes in the water. It was about proving I could do this – believing and achieving. The more I prepared for it, the more I thought it was going to be mine. I started to visualise myself walking around a new build. I saw the staff, the uniform, the students and the playground. I played the conversations I might have with Year 7 parents in my head as they stopped me at the front school gates – all of it imaginary at this time. I began to immerse myself in the role. I toyed with ideas of my vision and recruitment and I even did a few drives to where the school was planned to be located. I had worked my ass off and I had taken teaching and learning to the cusp of 'outstanding', bringing up the entire quality of education in the school and I had made a valuable contribution to leadership and management which was judged 'outstanding' in the last inspection. I was made. I was ready.

I was shortlisted and invited for an interview.

The interview was an absolute disaster. The following journal entry gives some detail and is probably helpful for those going for headships. Feel free to skip it, if the detail does not interest you, to get to the rest of the story, but I wanted to include it to share examples and give an insight into the process of a headship interview. Once you have made it through shortlisting and have been selected to be invited to interview, the interview usually takes place over two days, with Day 1 as the day of filtering the 'wheat from the chaff' – essentially, narrowing down the desired candidates. If you are invited back to Day 2, you have a good chance of getting the job.

First Headship Interview experience!

2 Mar 2017

I have just had my very first interview for a Principal Designate of a brand-new start-up free school. Before I elaborate, I feel the need to just quickly list some headlines:
- *Emotions before, during, after interview*
- *Post-mortem*
- *Reading*
- *Preparation*
- *The panels*
- *The support and encouragement*
- *Waiting*

• The phone call & 'I'll cut to the chase', phrases you might hear which indicate ...

The panels were:
(1) Guided conversation with DfE rep. and Chair of Governors Designate
(2) Teaching & Learning panel
(3) Finance & Marketing and
(4) Student panel. I was lucky to have two slots of free time at the end of the day, so it meant I could leave really early and go. Learning: what I would say/ do/ need to elaborate on in future: The guided conversation:
Firstly, let me just say that we were not told we would have this as one of the activities but it was good to have this as a warm-up. I was asked to talk through my journey to this point and not to do a presentation. I did go on a bit, I think, but that's the danger with these types of questions.

What are your expectations of me as Chair Designate?
What attracts you to this role?
Give examples of how you have worked with governors:
All in all, the conversation was down for 45 minutes but it probably took about 30 minutes.

The Teaching & Learning panel:

Teaching & Learning panel threw me!

What the hell! Given 20 minutes to read through data. It stated we had to identify the key issues within the data dashboard. Then inside, the task said to identify three areas of concern and what would I do in order to explore these concerns further before deciding on a course of action. In my mind, it was what I would consider before acting.

Once in the room, I was asked by one member to talk about the three areas of concern. I was not asked to do the second part so I was not sure if I should go into it straightaway or if I would be asked separately. This became very disjointed and the lady in the middle started rushing me! Rude! I was not clear on whether they wanted the key issues overall or just T&L. It did not specify for teaching and learning, so of course I identified issues including disadvantaged students, English teaching and SEN students with support. However, when I went into the panel, I had forgotten to write down my third point!!! So, I said behaviour for learning. I also made an error and said SEN students without support did worse – in fact, it was SEN students with support. I proceeded to fumble my way through answers. Can you believe it! My area of strength turned out to be my worst area.

How would you seek to engage with the community and the world of work?

In your first year, how would you best use the skills of staff in developing and improving the curriculum?
Well, it all went downhill from here! In my head, I translated this to mean using knowledge and expertise of teachers to build and introduce subjects which may be unusual or different. I did not think about it. I began to look at my notes and even my application! Shame! This took some time and I did not even come up stronger after that. I then asked for clarification three times on the question, as it was linked to curriculum and not T&L in the way I thought. She seemed to get irritated. They wrote only a few notes at that point ... how embarrassing.

Reflections on this panel:
Why are we made to feel stupid if we ask for questions to be rephrased? Could it be that they are not phrased well enough? Why are interviews made to be unnecessarily difficult as if that is part of the test? Is it not to judge if someone is good enough for the role? I personally think that interviews should not be the only way to recruit, certainly at this level, but to also have a way to see a snapshot of a person in action. There was a current serving headteacher, an ex-headteacher and also lead of this new school project and this dreadful woman, can't remember her name but she was quite curt and was also rushing me through. Why was she being this way with me? I had popped to the toilet for two minutes, which was right next to the room! Perhaps this was why she was rushing me???

Finance & Marketing panel:

This was always going to be a challenge. Even the deputy head competitor candidate (whose HT happened to be on this panel!) kept saying aloud: 'oh, finance, finance!!'). Not sure if that was some sort of psychological game he was playing ... but perhaps it worked? I can't see how he could be stuck when his own HT was heading up this panel. By the way, his school is outstanding.

The style of questions I was asked was not quite what I had been prepped for at NPQH or AHT level, and definitely not at my school.
Again, I had 20 minutes to look at documents: the first-year budget sheet for the school (alongside year 2 and 3 data) overall and the same for staffing costs. I was talked through and explained that if we only got 80% of the expected recruitment of students, we would have a deficit of −£197,360. Damn, where was my current finance lead when I needed him! I was not prepared at all.

What key changes would you make in year one following a 20% budget reduction due to fewer than expected student numbers? *And this is very REAL in the context of this new start-up school.*

I listed what I would reduce/ attempt to do. I tried my best to be creative with ideas. Firstly, I don't even know if these ideas were possible. Secondly, the fact that teachers might not sign up to my strategies and the lady on the panel made it obvious that she thought not too. Who does that on an interview panel? She said aloud, 'What? – teachers!?' with shock and horror, so I stuttered and said, 'Well, no, but support staff.' But hang on, there are only about three of those!

I was asked: 'So how much would all this save?'
Well, I hadn't done the maths, was I expected to? I had not done this – oh dear.

What would be your recruitment strategy?
Me: need the right people, in the right seats on the bus going in the direction of my vision, same direction. First would be seeking support from the Education Improvement Partnership

or EIP staff/ governors to recruit the School Business Manager or SBM to support me in the future decisions to be made about the rest of the recruitment and resources. Then my right-hand person – VP/ DHT, then core teachers. Eventually leading to recruitment of others and that I would want to sit at every recruitment interview. I said it may sound odd; she said, no that's normal, that's what we all do; and I said, well, I know heads who don't.

Student panel
This was the best part of the day. I came alive and really enjoyed speaking with them. They asked me:

- What makes a really good/ effective HT?
- Then came a Scenario – behaviour, mobile phones used to record a fight, big group of students – what would be my response?
- If you were an animal, what would you be and why?

I gave them two animals.
Panther – speed = efficiency and initiative, getting things done and being sleek like a panther, I went off on one about language college and benefits and being sleek and assemblies and setting up of tech. One girl said she hated that in assemblies her HT at primary would freeze board, go to laptop and then do other things. Irritated her! Oops.
Dove – peace = collaboration and everyone working with understanding. Importance in this current climate, them being the future, needing to work together.

- How would your personal friends describe you?
- What three words would you want the children to say about your school?
- What type of teachers do you want in your school?

I talked about relationships being positive, good teaching skills, able to manage behaviour, teach with passion, wanting to see children thrive and do their best, able to use a skill which is assessment for learning, and all staff to work well together.

There were other questions I cannot recall. The students wanted to talk to me and had questions additional to their listed questions. I was also given the opportunity to ask them questions. I asked why behaviour was important to them and what they looked for in a head: they said personality, connectedness with students, to have jokes, walk around, have presence and a passion for the job, allow them to grow in a safe environment. Brilliant answers.

Okay. Reflections. What are my gaps in knowledge? Finance, deficit, new start-up school, clear vision, articulating what kind of school I want more clearly, linking teaching and learning to data and talking about it succinctly. Talking like a headteacher and not like a deputy. Need coaching here.
I'm sure there are many more gaps.

Conclusion:
I am not left feeling proud of what I said and how I performed today. Even if not being invited to Day 2, at least I want to feel as though I showed potential and gave a good run for my competition, which included currently serving headteachers.

I started to write the following in my journal and then began to type things up, so the result is all of this now:

I feel a little sore. Do we ever feel we have answered correctly at interview? I found it a challenge. Had I discussed enough options for a new start-up school? Had I planned well enough the kind of school I wish to see? How can I be more precise in my answers? I didn't have much time to exercise the thinking role.

I felt my best area became my worst as I didn't sell enough of my knowledge of TLA. This was because they rushed me and I felt that the data task, although ultimately it all links to TLA, was better suited to talk about additional issues I could see within the data. I guess this is based on the training and development I am getting at my school.

> *I fumbled my way in …*
>
> *I came home and cried. I sent a text to my hubby. I then began to read Jill Berry's book* Making the Leap *(from DHT to HT!). Wish I had it earlier. Oh well, I will read it now so I can get ready. I tried to listen to a TED talk but couldn't. Felt tired and wanted to sleep but couldn't. Did not do much today. My HT had asked me this am if I wanted to attend a conference and speak alongside Aneeta Prem, the advocate of Freedom Charity for victims of forced marriage. I was charged up and immediately thought, great, yes, and replied so. I wish I hadn't. When I informed him I would be in the next day as I was not asked to go back, he said, 'Never mind — I am sure it was an interesting experience', then the next text read 'I will email you the conference stuff to cheer you up.' Odd. Why does he think this will do that?*
>
> *I rest my case.*
>
> *On a positive note: only my second application, and it made it to shortlisting out of 13 applicants to the final 6.*

Did you see that reframe? There was hope. My mental tenacity was developing. It was uncomfortable, but it was growth.

I was up against a colleague who I worked with at Willesden High, who was a current serving headteacher of five years and had worked in the borough as an adviser. She knew the deputy headteacher of one of the schools of the panel members.
This colleague was asked to return to Day 2. I texted her. Happy for her, she was good and deserving and I hoped she got it. She did. I felt really pleased that I knew her and her worth.

The other three candidates were men. One had already attended headteacher interviews.

In the meantime, I decided that my strategy would be to use support from my new-found network, which included my husband, my guardian angel, an ex-head, a current head and a leaving head, as well as anyone else willing.

A key part of going through any interview process, I feel, is getting the feedback and, no matter how harsh, understanding there may be some realities in it and working on the areas they mention. Even if they are not as bad as they seem – firstly, how do you know? Secondly, they have to give you the honour of feeding back on areas that stand out, so you can at least figure the areas mentioned were worth using to give feedback to you on. All the time, though, I have to admit there was a little voice thinking: 'Is it because I am Black?' Often, I closed it down, because if it was, thinking it alone at that time would get me nowhere. If anything, it made me determined to try to see if I could.

Feedback received from first Headship interview!!!

7 Mar 2017

It's 10:22 a.m. I have just come off the phone with Suzanne Walters at the headteacher recruitment firm. She was lovely and asked me, as I knew she would, what I thought about the interview and how I felt things went. I gave her my synopsis of not selling myself enough and not being strong enough in the finance panel and finally not being able to articulate what was required for the teaching and learning panel. I felt that I did well at the student panel and okay in the DfE/ Chair panel.

She said I was definitely self-aware and spot on with my self-review as this was pretty much what was said.

It was a tough panel. She had never seen one with so many serving heads on it! She also said it was a very strong field and I came across as very confident and with lots of professionalism and that I am forward-thinking.

Finance: I struggled here, but came across stronger when talking about staff recruitment.

T&L panel: In summing up, there seems to have been a mismatch with what they were looking for and what I was thinking they were looking for. Felt there was much more there but I did not articulate it.

Student panel: I was very popular with the student panel.

DfE/ Chair panel: I did not sell myself enough, did not give as much detail in responses.

Biggest area to focus on is finance and I am not alone! Attending committees, seeing how the budget is managed from HT view would be helpful. This is the big step up from DHT to HT.

There was not a single person who said they did not see me as a head and they saw headship potential in me. BINGO!

I quote, she said:

'I don't know what your relationship is with your head, but you should ask for opportunities to attend as an observer, work with them as they set the budget ...'

I will ask. Let's see how that goes.

> *I then was bolshie enough to say that I noticed there was a job going at the neighbouring school and if anything came up that she should feel free to contact me. She talked about the possibility of trying to attract a serving head but she knew many of them would be asking themselves 'what's in it for me?' especially as it is a Requires Improvement, grade 3, school and if they are coming from 'good' schools they may not see the point in going there. She finished by saying that if I was shortlisted for this school, it was definitely worth looking into as I was a strong candidate ...*
>
> *Don't they always say that bit??? Maybe not – I suppose if I was not ready they would say that too, perhaps.*
>
> *I'll request a pack and have a look at it from there.*

That was my playtime. I did honestly know I didn't have a hope in hell, but it was a good way of testing the waters, dipping my toe in and seeing how deep I had to dive.

By the time I was going for the headship for real, I had gone past worrying about what everyone else was thinking. I was done with second-guessing myself, doubting myself, wondering if I was worth it, good enough or should even believe I could. I thought I could, so I did. Just like the campaign says.

Interview number 2
Two years later, I had the interview at school number 2. I was not called back for Day 2, but this time it was a very positive experience.

This is the content of my journal from my Day 1 application:

> *Today I was told I wouldn't be invited back to Day 2 of a headship interview once again. It is really disappointing*

> *and disheartening. This year I've had to contend with a health scare, the loss of a dear friend, tiredness, and unsuccessful yet extremely draining headship applications and interview processes. I'm fed up, but I know my time will come.*

Interview number 3

I had no chance. Up against the only other candidate, who was an internal. I did not have enough intel. If I had, I would never have gone for it. It turned out this school had been abandoned by a headteacher who had gone AWOL and another executive head had been asked to take it on. She did, reluctantly, and as any good head would do, she used it as an opportunity to further one of her team who got the position. I was there to make up a 'field' so they could go through the process. It was so clear once I found out. My advice from this experience would be to do your background checks as much as you can into those running the process as much as into the school.

The appointed colleague – a white male.

Interview number 4

All I can say here is the chair of governors loved me, as did I her. Not romantically, of course, but we could definitely have worked together and I saw deep sorrow in her eyes when she bade me farewell. It was strange. Clearly, there were factors beyond her control keeping her from deciding to employ me. Same sort of rigmarole of questions and panels. Same outcome again. The irony – it was the neighbouring school to school number 1.

Whatever the key take-away from each interview, it's important to hold onto something positive and, even though it may hurt to hear it, something you can take away and improve on. For me it was galvanising.

The appointed colleague – a white male.

The feedback I received to date included comments such as 'excellent feedback from the staff', 'clearly ready to take on the headship', 'wanted to take forward a candidate who had already been a head', 'students really engaged and liked you' and the interview was 'really impressive'.

Interview number 5: My dream school

29 Nov 2018

My dream school to lead has just slipped away from me. Just took a call from the chair of governors who said that, unfortunately, they were not going to offer me the job. They had very long deliberations but they have settled on another candidate.

He said he would give feedback in due course. He said that I performed well and that he is sure I will make an excellent headteacher soon – he is sure it won't be long.

The question is whether or not I want to go for it again. Once again, I need time to recover, reflect and make a decision.

So one of the questions I was asked was 'why Nower Hill?' and why now? I had an answer prepared for this which was they would be in need of a strong HT with experience of leading schools to outstanding and I had the right skill set but I don't think I put it across quite like this. They asked me about data skills and I wonder if this was the question I did not answer well enough.

It was to put down three strengths and areas for development and I only put down two, so perhaps these things worked against me. When asked about where data would sit, I said probably an area to develop as I always feel I need to develop in this area.

Oh well, huge thanks to everyone supporting me through this process.

Interview number 6

By this time, I could see, feel and hear myself being the headteacher. I walked around the school assuming I would confidently beat my opponents and lead this wonderful school. It was close, very close, and I could feel the fear beginning to rise as I realised how successful I was becoming. Once again, I was up against an internal candidate and, once again, I saw the look in the eyes of the governing body that said – 'We'll stick with what we know.'

The appointed colleague – a white male.

I am sure you see the pattern emerging here with the colleagues who were appointed.

Interview number 7

Not every school is the school for you, but when you are going for something, it becomes hard at times to see this. I was glad, later on, that I was unsuccessful for this position. Let's say, I dodged a bullet. I learned the school had a deficit and was impossible to manage.

My experience with the 15-large governing body panel was a mixture of fun, nerves and bewilderment. There were some members of the panel who were there only in body, as they were silent whilst the interview was dominated by a few who did their best job of grilling me for 90 minutes.

One interesting question though was 'Is there anything on social media that we should be aware of which could compromise you?'

Being who I am, I looked at each one, in turn, took an extended pause and then said, 'Well, actually, no.'

You should have seen the look on their faces. I wanted to burst out laughing. It was as if they were not expecting me to say 'no' but were not prepared if I had said 'yes' either. I had taken a risk – but it had worked – it was a way to lighten up the interview a bit and we laughed as one of them said, 'Phew!' That was because I had done very well and they saw hope in me.

I was once again called back for Day 2, meaning I was definitely getting good at demonstrating my skills and being recognised as a school leader. It wasn't to be.

The appointed colleague – a white male.

After this, I saw no point in trying. I just felt it was not worth it and would not happen.

I remember having a conversation with one of my guardian angels who was pushing me to say what I really thought was going on but I just could not, up until this point. I finally succumbed and said, 'I'll be honest, I do wonder if in UK education they just do not want a Black and female headteacher leading schools.'

I just could not see what else it could be. I had refined my responses. I had come second so many times and had worked to address all the areas of development, so much so that I was performing in some areas more strongly than in teaching and learning, my passion. This is why the saying, 'You have to work twice as hard' resonates with members of the Black community, as that is how it feels.

If there is a meritocracy then why were my skills always falling short? Laughing with me, smiling with me, placating me did not a headteacher in me make. I was done with the late nights, the lack of sleep on top of the exhausting energy taken out of me and the need to recover for a week after going to interviews whilst doing my current role.

A key point to note, however, is the interview is as much for them, the panellists, as it is for you and as one of my connections said to me, 'The right school will find you and you will find it.'

Interview number 8 – I did it!

On 28 April 2019, I attended a new church for the very first time. Interestingly, the pastor was a childhood friend who had known me for years. It was interesting because never in our childhood years would we probably ever have imagined meeting at a church.

My church experience as a child was blighted by my childhood trauma and attending Pentecostal churches where individuals would sometimes scream and shout. They said that they were in the Holy Spirit, but it scared me and did not make for an easy church experience. It instilled in me a lot more fear and added to the feelings of an already anxious child. I never really bought into it, sensing that some were overly 'spiritual', making it a competition of who could shout the loudest.

Nevertheless, through my husband's journey which returned him to his faith, I too had gently been encouraged to return to seek a place in my heart for God's word. It also brought me to test out this new church led by Minister Alex. At this service, Minister Alex called me out to say a few words.

My worst nightmare.

Whilst as a leader I speak and address hundreds of young people and even maybe large groups of staff at a time, my presence in church is totally different. I like to be unnoticed and literally take the back seat. However, all I could do was respectfully obey his request. After I greeted the church, he spoke about his desire for me to become a headteacher, a leader in the community, and of how proud he would be, not 'if' but 'when' I reach the goal. He did not even know I had completed seven applications already.

Minister Alex prayed over me in a way no one had ever done before. It was heartfelt, genuine and full of good wishes and blessings.

On 24 May 2019, I was appointed as headteacher of Rooks Heath College, a 1,200-student, large secondary school in West London.

Two weeks before this, my guardian angel had pointed me in the direction of headship positions on offer and instead of just searching in the *TES* (the widely acknowledged teacher newspaper) I looked in *The Guardian* as well.

He continued to tell me that there was a school out there for me. Every school needed to be the right fit for me as I did for them, and the others possibly fell short of these criteria. I looked through the headteacher adverts in *The Guardian* paper and there it was, in my ideal location, right by my home, and also type of school. I downloaded the application form and put it on the dining table to complete that weekend.

When I lifted the pen to write my ideas down, I became overwhelmed. The feelings of exhaustion and the potential rejection once more resigned me to give in. I took one more look over all the information that lay before me, all the tabs I had opened to research the school, the history, the community, the areas I felt less confident in, the Ofsted report and whatever else and then I kissed my teeth and slowly began to tear the paperwork, including the freshly printed application form, in two. I was done. I could not put myself through this again. It would be too much to bear. Plus, I was getting dangerously too close to the number 13, like one of my previous headteachers had done. I had said that it meant I was not cut out to be a school leader.

What was I thinking? Look at who I am. I was trying too hard and, clearly, I was not what schools wanted or needed. Forget it.

I anticipated that the two-day pattern before the completion of the interview, where I would shed a tear, get palpitations and be full of anguish before I was able to reframe this into excitement, would just do me in.

I can only say that my husband is definitely the one for me. At this moment, he was the ally I needed. This was the agency required. The mentor, the coach, the one with belief in me. As I said, everyone deserves a champion. Surrounding yourself with them means they can have your back at any time. I was lucky that it was my husband. For others, this ally can manifest in anyone you trust and whose opinions and actions you value.

With a temper like mine, he still decided to go into our bin (it's okay, it was the dry paper recycling bin) and recover the torn application form and the paperwork I had printed off. Luckily, I had not decimated the paper into tiny bits – how I normally would. He laid it on the dining table again. He had been watching and knew exactly how I laid out my research and activities in readiness to prepare my application.

When I returned to the dining table and saw them there, I was confused at first. I looked at Theo; he was sitting, as usual, comfortably on the sofa, watching the footy. He had assumed the very same position. To be honest, that wasn't hard! I couldn't believe he had done that. Rather than rant and cuss him off and ask why? I simply sat down, took a long deep breath and restarted the process. It was worth it. Little did I know that this school would be the right fit.

****

Those words, those words, those words. 'We would like to offer you the post.'

… I was finally going to have a seat at the headteacher's table and taste the elixir of equality.

From Hood to Headship

I came home, kicked off my comfy Clarks 'interview day' shoes and slumped on the couch. I stared at my mobile for what seemed like ages before finding the energy to pick it up and catch up on my WhatsApp messages and emails. Amongst them was the text message received from Kay. Kay's text was a reminder that today was the memorial of my best friend in my first three years of secondary school. I cried. I cried as I looked at the picture. I cried as I searched for other pictures to use to also remind myself and others of the loss of this beautiful soul. And I cried because I was simply exhausted.

I had just returned from the seventh headship interview, the third for this academic year alone. Just as I was about to get up to grab a cup of tea, the phone rang.

'Oh, hello, is that Miriam?'

'Yes,' I responded.

'Oh, Jack and Jill would like to ask if you could pop back in – a strange request, but they hoped you would be able to do this as they'd like to speak with you in person.'

'Okay,' I responded, 'I'll make my way back.'

My heart pounded, my stomach gave a small twist, my legs stood me up and I went to my car and drove back to the school. When I arrived at the school, not only were Jack and Jill waiting but two more from the panel earlier. Dan and Pat were there as well. I couldn't contain it and blurted out that I was sorry, but my body was nervous and trembling as I didn't anticipate what they were about to tell me.

'Well, we thought it would be best to have you return and speak to us as you don't live too far away – we hope that is okay.'

I nodded, my throat began to do that 'I'm drying up' thing and I instinctively caught it and my brain told my throat, 'Not yet ... wait for it.'

'Well, we have come to a decision after discussing your performance today, and we'd like to offer you the post.'

What? Did she just say 'offer you the post'? Yessssss, she sure did. A sigh of relief, a brief moment of 'I'm going to cry', which I verbalised only to be warned by Jack that I'd set him off too if I did, and then a hot flush. But my palms weren't sweaty and I felt fine. It then dawned on me ... I have finally arrived. I have finally achieved my first headship. I did it.

Part 3

Headship

14. Let the first 100 days begin!

'Enjoy your achievements as well as your plans.

Keep interested in your own career, however humble; it is a real possession in the changing fortunes of time.'

(Max Ehrmann, 1927)

Attention, senior leaders and fellow headteachers. I have an announcement to make. Home life carries on! Just because I was in senior leadership and I had spent the best part of my life, let alone the summer holidays, preparing for this moment, did not mean the world stood still for me in order to do so. As much as we may feel powerful as leaders, we think we have the power, but in fact, life has the power. It makes us remember that family matters. Balancing the demands of parenthood with activities which are interspersed between the commitment of work duties has just become a way of life for me, as I am sure it is for many.

30 Aug 2019
It's 17:36. I have just had a massive row with hubby due to what I consider his 'lack of consideration and empathy' for the new head who is preparing this weekend. After having had a splendid celebration of 10 years of marriage, I felt like this was about to put it all to bed! Well, indeed, we had a wonderful 4 weeks in Ghana, with friends and family. All was going swimmingly well ... until ... the daughter asks if we can have a BBQ at our house. When I asked 'Why?' I was met with 'What's the problem? It's only a BBQ and if we don't do it now, then when?'

> *Well, first there is the fact that we are not even back in the UK. Then there is the fact that, when I return, I literally hit the ground running, going in on exam results day (probably my fault for booking such a tight flight, although there was not even a headship interview on the horizon when I did!) and then I need to visit not one but both schools, old first of course, then new. It seemed to make sense to me to do it in that order. Then there is the issue that we have just spent a colossal amount of money whilst abroad and this will bring on additional unplanned expenditure, of course. Oh yes, and finally, that I will literally be in day 1 of the 100 days of headship if I count it from this week. Plus, to top it off, I am as nervous as hell.*

All roads led in a tunnel vision to 'my' new school, 'my' new job, 'my priorities', everything of 'me'. Everything I thought about was around my hopes, aspirations and intentions when in the new school. I simply could not wait. I set dates to meet with the most significant people I needed to straightaway and was not taking 'no' for an answer when requesting the time to do this at my current school. Knowing the potential battle I would face to have this granted, I would take the time unpaid if I needed to, without any hesitation. I was eager and keen to start. It was amazing how achieving this new role had given me the strength and focus to not even consider the 'what ifs'. No one could say anything to me to destroy my high at this point.

Still, there was room for self-doubt to sneak in, a crack in my new-found armour. In spite of the hill I had climbed and walked down, this next experience highlights how deeply seated my resentment and fear were, as I immediately resorted to those negative thoughts and silently lobbed them onto my unsuspecting and of course completely innocent new employers!

He's not in

25 June 2019

Tuesday 25 June 2019 – no meetings, don't go in.

Well, I am sat here frustrated, angry actually at not being able to go into my new school. It must have moved me so much as it has propelled me into the seat to journal about it. I was so looking forward to going in and seeing how they do things at the two meetings. There isn't much time left and I am navigating both my current work, the planning for Ghana and going into the new job – this is the lead-in period. I want to give myself the best chance of doing the job well. Got a call this morning at 7:30 a.m. or so, which I missed, from the school. Only to receive a text saying that, as the outgoing head, Benjamin, was unwell, he wouldn't be in and it would be more beneficial for me to come another day. Perhaps it is because of my experience with my head, Phil, but it ignited in me all sorts of emotions and thoughts. Have they had second thoughts? Was I a bit full-on at the headteacher's conference, leading to him wanting to control more my involvement with the school, even though he has stated very clearly that he will be hands off? Have I given an impression of being too forward and already inciting fear and change, all because I have planned and organised the days I wish to come into the school, and also meet with members of the SLT just for a chat? Perhaps, I gave too much away, telling Benjamin and Oliver, the associate head, what I would be talking to the SLT about, but I wanted to be open, I've nothing to hide.

It has angered me but getting this down in my journal has helped. I will now return to Greenleaves. I have loads to do anyway. That is part of the problem. Up till late trying

> *to finish the last of my Spanish marking at Greenleaves, the Year 10 exam papers, and also trying to read my books on headship as well as take in information about the new school. Jill Berry (Berry, 2016) could not have described this lead-in period better in terms of the toll it takes psychologically when making the leap to headship. I am filled with excitement and the urgency to get myself ready, especially as I got the post at the end of May. Yet I have to remain circumspect and heedful and not overstep the mark as I am not the head yet, but a head-in-waiting. The current head, who is a larger-than-life character already, is very much in control.*
>
> *So, I guess I can only do what I can from my end and, whatever they allow me to do, I will. I can't help but think they are fearful of something and don't want me there today. It could however simply be what it is, that he is unwell and not in. To be fair, at the residential, there was mention of him having to check himself out due to some medical issue which I didn't quite catch.*
>
> *I guess I can count my blessings in that I can do some productive work today instead.*

What a load of tosh!

I can truly sincerely say that I could not have been more wrong. I was blessed with this ex-head being a CEO (Chief Executive Officer) of a great Trust and school that I had inherited when I took over as head.

I have heard about new heads getting into roles, particularly in Trusts, and the relationships with CEOs being of a different kind and in some cases destructive and detrimental. Lucky for me, my context presented a different scenario.

Every job I am about to embark on I bring at least one fear. School one, the fear that I would not actually succeed as a teacher and not have other strings to my bow. School two, the fear of not living up to the expectation of leading a headteacher and a deputy headteacher in my department; and school four, a fear of leading whole school assemblies – I had not done this very much up to this point and I knew they would be par for the course. It was like getting a new car and each time noticing what features you had, then saving up to get an improved newer model – each model having something good to work with, but some feature missing that needed to be added next time. It was the opposite in my job – each fear decreased and paled into insignificance as I grew and developed. On becoming a headteacher, once again my paradigm shifted and with it came a new fear.

My one fear this time was of my leadership team. Who would they be? Would they listen to me? Would they respect me? Would they get along? What sort of lion's den would I be going into? How about my deputy heads, especially the pastoral one – would they match my values on children and my purpose to meet their every need? Would they fully grasp the need to understand my passion for children and that I would not be the sort of head to rush to resort to excluding any child for any misdemeanour, unless there was no other way?

From Hood to Headship

Image: iStock.com/ XiXinXing.

From my reading, I could see that the critical time frame for anyone starting afresh in a new establishment was 90–100 days. Literally, there are books entitled *The First 90 Days* or *The First 100 Days*. The question for me was where this would begin. In my mind, I had always thought of the first 100 days as starting from the day after being accepted for the post (just to give myself more time, plus I like the sound of 100). However, it goes without saying that, in the minds of many others, it starts from day one, as you walk on site to your new place of work, in my scenario, the school. In reality, though, I feel that the first 100 days begin somewhere in between.

Such was my experience. Whilst I have journaled my feelings on the moment I was told, 'We would like to offer you the post', and whilst I had from that day on anxious thoughts about my first day on site, the first 100 days felt like they began for me on that GCSE results morning. That very day that I decided to fly back to London and walked into the new school as the head designate, to meet with my predecessor, discuss a little bit about how the GCSE results day procedures went, and touch on the exam results.

As my luck would have it, for the first time in the three-year trend for the school since the introduction of the Progress 8 measure, the way schools are judged on how well they help students make progress towards good GCSE exam grades, the school had slipped into a negative progress score. This indicated that students were making less than positive progress and in fact were going backwards. I knew then, interesting times lay ahead. It would be up to me to get the school back into the positive Progress 8 figures it had previously celebrated.

Because I was undecided about when to begin the 100 days, in my anal kind of way, I decided to plot what I wanted to achieve at the end of *three* sets of 100 days.

I used this site to work these out (you didn't think I sat there counting them, did you?): https://www.convertunits.com/dates/100/daysfrom/May+24,+2019 (ConvertUnits.com, n.d.)

My diary entry read as follows:

> *100 days from appointment = 1 September 2019*
> *100 days from GCSE day = 30 November 2019*
> *100 days from Monday 2 September 2019 = 11 December 2019*
>
> *Goals:* **100 days from appointment** *= 1 September 2019: Key SLT members met, PA met, key individuals met, moved into office, first letter to parents completed and shared, first speech to staff prepared, ready to be delivered, website has new image and welcome message uploaded. Main IT systems known, first two weeks of activities scheduled, results known and whole school*

priorities clear, organisation of SLT roles and line management structure in draft form at least.

Most of this was already completed by today; however, some barriers encountered ... first of all, there is no single person responsible for the marketing! Website and communications are done by a few people and seem very ad hoc. Hello! We need to raise the profile of this lovely school. This should be paramount. No Twitter or LinkedIn either. I think they are missing a trick here, so I wish to get this up and running as well. They use Facebook, oddly, as this I feel is better suited for reaching out to alumni.

*Goals: **100 days from GCSE day** = 30 November 2019*

At the time of writing this first entry (30 Aug 2019), I have gotten as far as having an idea of what I wish to achieve overall but not up to this date. Still time to think and I will come back to writing here after today. Perhaps one thing should be done – the appraisal system completed.

*Goals: **100 days from first day in school – Monday 2 September 2019** = 11 December 2019*

Quick wins established as follows: new lanyards for staff, birthday cards to every staff member who has had a birthday this term, Open Evening successfully organised, website refreshed with new head images, results, events, parent newsletters and student voice newsletters and/or safeguarding newsletters, new table tennis tables, establishment of SLICT group (Strategic Leadership of ICT – name borrowed from previous school), organised meetings, agreement on single ICT software for admin, data and assessment including homework and parent liaison.

It's been an interesting week following the August Bank Holiday. I have continued meeting staff since I began the process in June. It went something like this:

Tuesday 27 August 2019

10 a.m. met with the CEO, lasted about 2.5 hours, worthwhile as we went through the quagmire of staffing.

The rest of the day, I tried to use the IT systems to organise my materials and made a start on the SLT responsibilities documents. Difficult when not knowing the nuances of the individuals but helped by using documents I had accumulated previously and cross-referencing with the information given to me by the new school's 'walking encyclopaedia' ... who has just retired after an amazing 45 years at the school! Okay, so I guess he deserves to retire ... but now???
He is an amazing source of all information, which he has taken with him.

3:20 p.m. left and took son 1 to the opticians (still being mummy).

Came home, unable to ring a colleague at another school who wanted to speak to me about headship search and other things, meant to be at 3:30 p.m. but phone had died. Time flew by and then I had to do an interview for a friend's PhD dissertation about Blackness and Whiteness from 6 p.m. which went over to 7:15 p.m.! Was meant to collect son 2 from basketball, but whilst on the call, hubby comes in, steals car and son 1 (to go to rugby it turns out) and leaves! Luckily, he was able to get son 2 or I would have been up the creek without a paddle.

Finally, I called my coach.

Wednesday 28 August 2019

Went into new school for around 9 a.m. Tried to do some bits. Interestingly, I spent a lot of time ... talking ... a lot. It was good. I got the feeling that not much work was being done by anyone, the PA, the CFO or me. But it was all school business ... mostly. More importantly, a crucial part of the work – we were bonding. Conversations were varied and very deep. I was told about a multitude of different histories, encounters, things they expected and hoped for – most of all, their hopes. No pressure then, I thought. They are a lovely bunch and really looking forward to working with them. However, I came home and thought, I need a code. Yes, door closed, DO NOT DISTURB.

11:40 a.m. left to take sons to dentist. Returned to work for a bit longer; again, it felt like I had not done much. It wasn't true, I just wanted to be super speedy through my ever-extending 'to-do' list. I wanted to do some data analyses and prepare the SLT responsibilities document which needed some thinking through; it just seemed to be taking me ages. I had also been accosted by several staff members wanting to talk to me – including one in particular who took up too much of my time. I learned she wanted more pay, or had been promised a teaching and learning responsibility pay point (TLR) by previous HT ... managed to defer her to Friday. A taste of things to come?

4 p.m. took my boys to my sister's, as I felt really guilty. It is after all still their holiday time. Returned home to have nails done at 5:30 p.m., then came home and collapsed in my chair. I was mentally exhausted already.
Got dressed at 7:30 p.m. and went to salsa! Oh yes, indeed. I had missed 4 weeks, I needed to unleash.

Thursday 29 August 2019

Went in at 7:50 a.m. to meet my PA. We spent a little over an hour. Extremely well worth it. She is simply awesome, not quite like Donna from the US series Suits *(Korsch, 2011) but on the way. Learnt about her, how she works and that she will organise my life! No joke! I am not used to this ... but I can be. How wonderful.*

9:30 – 1 p.m. met with the Chief Financial Officer (CFO) who is also the Director of Business. Oh, what a meeting. The great thing is she had the agenda. A long list which complemented and supplemented all the things I wanted to speak about. I also liked that she had the courage to share with me a detail from my interview. She prefaced it with,
'You know you said you like honesty and that's how I hope that we can continue.'
Naturally, I was a little unnerved. But then she shared that she had been the only one on the panel with a negative to say, and that negative was that she noted

that finance was not my strength! Is that all? I thought. Well, excuse me, but 'you were right' – I told her:
'It isn't and I knew you noted this. I think this is great as I won't make any decisions before checking with you. I also know that I have great strengths in the core business of the school, the teaching and learning, so we will work well together.'

I was completely fine with this. I loved her honesty.

Friday 30 August 2019

In at 8:20 a.m. I had a meeting scheduled for 9 a.m. but by the time I did the 'hello's again with my ladies, it was already 8:30 a.m., my next appointment was already in the foyer and waiting, she had a chat with the CFO and then came to meet with me. We had a 2-hour meeting about data, and a package to analyse it called SISRA but this still did not give me all I wanted. I know it was because of time and she did go through everything. I just wanted to have in my hand some data for the middle leaders, the Heads of subject Departments. It has been sent, so I will just have to work things out and not be frustrated that I don't have the same systems in place as we did at my previous school. I was grateful to her, though – another one who after 42 years of being there was delivering her swan song to help me!

*Had an excellent meeting with the third and newly appointed DHT (deputy headteacher). Allowed me to finalise changes to names and number of meetings!! I decided to change the acronym STRP (pronounced funnily as 'strip') team from Short Term Review and Planning to **ST**rategic **R**eview and **P**lanning **T**eam. SLT to Leadership*

Forum and SP to SLG – Strategic Leadership Group – with a focus on logistics.

A very funny critical incident today and a bit of frustration of the highest order when the very efficient SENCo decided to create me a business Google account using my email address which I had done already with Google, so this overtook my Google account, causing a pause of 90 minutes in my day as we all tried to figure out how to ensure nothing was lost and I could use the diary. When I summoned him to my office, I could see he felt really bad, slightly red in the cheeks, and seemed uncertain about what I was going to say. So I softened it by saying I could see that he was 'über' efficient. He quickly learned how skilled and adept I am at using IT, though, I can tell you. Probably unlike my lovely predecessor? Maybe. He did me a favour, though, as the battle of 'where do I save my stuff?' is now over!

Came home at 4 p.m. Not ideal, leaving my son 2 at home all day alone whilst the other son went to the Roundhouse in Camden to get some studio music-playing time. Good for him and his mate.

So now I am going to play basketball with son 2 to make up for my time at work and de-stress.

Lots to do, family day tomorrow which I would rather not have but hey, heads to plait too and speech to go through, data sheet to prepare and still the SLT roles. Oh well, it will need to be done between tonight and Sunday.

Let the basketball playing begin ... as the 100 days roll on!

My pre-headship reading had paid off. My plan of action had begun and the 'three-questions' one-to-one meetings I had begun, starting with my leadership team, allayed all of my many fears. This was one of the strategies I gleaned from Jill Berry's 'bible' for aspiring heads, *Making the Leap*, which I would strongly recommend to everyone at this stage of their career. It was a great feat and I would need to do this with 168 staff in total but it would be worth it. I would gain an insight into the school, get a feel for individuals, as they would for me, and set the stall out on my vision and expectations for the school.

When I think about the relationships I have built now and the way in which I have been shown complete welcome, given authority and respect, I know that I was completely brainwashed and mistaken. I made the mistake of judging people by the actions of others. Thankfully, this was short-lived and I also trained the mind to reframe and change my thought paradigm, mainly by lots of self-talk and having those key individuals to touch base with. Sometimes we need to step back and ask ourselves what we know to be true. Actions speak louder than words and they had done. My concerns were misplaced, and I had nothing to worry about. I just needed to lead my school as well as I could.

The realisation that I was the headteacher came during one of my visits to the school. As I jollied about my new office, playing my Afro Beats playlist on Spotify, making it mine and leaving my stamp on it, changing the wall hangings, rearranging some of the visible shelving and clearing out the floor-to-ceiling cabinets, I was jolted out of my moment with a knock at the door.

I looked up and there stood a colleague who asked, 'Lily has asked if she will be paid, as she needs to leave to pick her son up early three days next week.'

Immediately, I began to turn around and look behind me. No kidding! I was actually considering passing up the question and asking the next person up. There was no 'next person up'. That person was me. I had to decide and provide the staff member with an outcome.

Wow. There it was. The recognition that the buck really did stop with me. I was the ultimate decision-maker. The greatest change from being a deputy head has been exactly that, making even more high-level decisions. This has taken me some time to get used to and, even now, there are times when I stop and take stock of this. Seeing myself as the little girl from Harlesden will always make me humble, but I remind myself that I deserve to be where I am. I worked hard for this and I am credible.

The first day of term in September, at the school gates, I met a lovely student first thing who greeted me so nicely. He remembered me from the summer term assemblies, asked me how my holidays went and wished me a good day. I also saw him at the end of the day. Pleasant students like this make all the difference. I can honestly say that the majority of students were very pleasant and greeted me warmly. At the gate, I also met the likes of Elias. I confiscated his cherry coke and he started to square up to me.

'Oh really?' I thought.

I just stood still, square on. I could see he was a little surprised.

'Do you know who I am?' I asked.

He put on his most menacing face, and said, 'No, who are you?'

'I'm your new headteacher and, if you want to get along, I suggest you stop trying to be a bad man and hand me the bottle, go about your business, and I wish you a good term.'

Elias took a moment to think, handed me the bottle and disappeared. He could clearly see from my tone that I was not one to be messed about with.

The academic year 2019–2020 was a year of varied firsts and lasts, as exemplified by the following journal entry.

My 'Firsts' and 'Lasts'

1 July 2019

As I prepare to empty my mind of the Greenleaves way in preparation for my headship at Ertha Hooks High school, I realise that there will be many things I begin to do for the first time and also my last. Here is a record of my firsts and lasts which I will update as time goes on:

Thursday 27 June – led the panel of my last interview and recruitment for my current school and appointment of the successful candidate.

Monday 1 July – my first Year 5 Taster Day organised and first time ever in the new school.

Monday 1 July – my last online PD activity deadline to staff as Safeguarding Lead – to complete Prevent training.

Thursday 4 July – my first address to the New Intake of Year 7 (currently Year 6) for September 2019 and their parents; this will be jointly with the outgoing headteacher. I have already typed up the speech I plan to deliver.

Friday 5 July – my last mark book entry of exam marks for a class at my current school – for my Year 10 Spanish group.

Thursday 11 July – use of my last diary page at current school.

Monday 15 July – held my first assembly with all the students from Years 7–10 in a row! Exhausting.

Tuesday 16 July – my last-ever lesson. It was with Year 10 Spanish and I had just done a celebration assembly with them where I sang 'Despacito' with a colleague, then did a solo of 'The Greatest Love of All' in front of the whole year group. The lesson was short but sweet. Also the 'last supper' with the SLT – we went to Blue Ginger and I was presented with a card and also a £150 Amazon voucher – great way to get fit so I can start by purchasing the much-avoided Fitbit. Good stuff. A pleasant evening though I wasn't ready to do a full-on speech, so I read my first entry from this journal and also said a few thank-yous. Not many! Said I would save it for Friday!

My first letter to parents was posted yesterday. I did this after painstakingly rethinking what I wanted to say, combined with a little help from The Key for School Leaders (Key, n.d.) and one other random headteacher's letter to parents, just to get a flavour of what I felt I should include.

My first speech to the staff at my new school. I think I have finalised it now and will be delivering this on Monday 2 September. As I write this, it is Friday 30 August, after spending most of the day there.

I've had …

My first address to parents.

My first assembly to all year groups.

My first permanent exclusion hearing – how interesting it was to not be contributing but a leading figure amongst those present in the hearing. You realise how much you have the fate of a child in your hands. Some say 'we can't save them all' and, sadly, this seems true.

My first Heads' meeting – with all the secondary headteachers in the borough. What are the chances of landing a job that gives this opportunity? Bonus!

My first investigation … of staff … all part of the job.

My first angry parent in reception … I was ready for them!

My first Pay Review Panel meeting with governors. The exiting headteacher did it as part of our handover time.

My first Parents, Teachers and Friends Association (PTFA) meeting with parents – from 6 to 7 p.m. … with a total of … drum roll … two parents and presided over by one Head of Year. What a shame about attendance but it was really good. I was able to give a condensed, more reduced version of the governor report I had prepared, which they found useful and I received some good feedback on my fireworks warning letter and on how Year 7 are settling in!

The goal now is to get more parents to attend!!! I must do a parents' newsletter …

… And this I completed and sent out at the end of term!

My first parent 'new' newsletter completed, yay! Thursday 19 December. My stamp on the new style.

My first whole staff end-of-term lunch. Thursday 19 December.

My first staff Christmas do – Thursday 19 December – and what a do. What a blessing to see the staff REALLY, I mean REALLY, letting their hair down. I had a great time too and it is very telling by those who attended where the heart of the school is. Those who work hard, heart and soul, were those I identified there. Not saying that others don't, but for example, the absence of teams that were constantly unsettled and had less collegiality amongst themselves was very obvious to me.

The weakest team (in terms of academic outcomes for students) was also absent – interestingly, neither of those teams I am having to deal with regarding staff relationships and timetable issues! I just feel that having balance is really important and, whilst I said at first, I would not go as I wanted the staff to feel at ease without fear of what the new headteacher would think, listening to my coach, that would not be truly me. I have decided that I am going to be true to me. Be my authentic self. I like people and I like socialising, even if I am shy at times, and I am glad I went. I showed that I am also human and able to 'get down' and enjoy time with others. Listen, if the CEO can be there, merry and having a good time, so can I!

Like Justin Timberlake's refrain of the McDonald's advert, I was 'just loving it'. My school. My students. My staff. My purpose. One term down and looking forward to the many to come.

Shortly came the end of term one and the end of the second set of 100 days.

15. Beyond the first 100 days

'And whatever your labours and aspirations, in the noisy confusion of life, keep peace in your soul. With all its sham, drudgery and broken dreams, it is still a beautiful world. Be cheerful. Strive to be happy.'

(Max Ehrmann, 1927)

There have been so many occasions where I have come home feeling a sense of achievement, taking things off my to-do list and feeling as though I am making real progress. But one of the frustrations of being a very new headteacher is you feel as though the world is watching you make a massive impact but you don't feel you are making the impact quickly enough. You are hoping to make a huge difference, because that's what you've been placed there to do. But Rome was not built in a day.

As a Black headteacher, that weight has a few more dumbbells added – the weight of the expectations of your own people. I would hear it in passing, in parental comments, in expressions of interest and awe. On receiving emails laced with phrases like '... in a school that is supposed to be inclusive and celebrate cultural diversity you should ...' and such-like, when parents needed to vent about the injustices that they perceived came from the education system. I would hear it too in the raising of eyebrows as individuals met me or were introduced to me, in the glances and looks; it was audible even if at those times those giving the glances thought it was silently conveyed.

A great irritation of mine was the feeling that I was taking one step forward and two steps back every time.

There were several occasions when I would come home and feel overwhelmed with all the things I was hoping to accomplish, feeling I had accomplished none of them.

I recall having a conversation with a headteacher when this individual had been appointed and was about a year into post. I remember asking, 'How are you feeling now it's nearly a year into headship? How are things going?' He replied that he sometimes found it frustrating because he had a momentum and a pace at which he wanted to see change, and yet often others didn't go at that pace and he felt that things were coming along too slowly. Boy, do I relate to that now!

One of the sad parts of headship is when the buck really stops with you regarding the premature end of a student's time at your school. Sadly, I had to lead my first permanent exclusion meeting within two weeks of beginning. Then another a month later. I was not expecting that. We can't save them all. I wish I could. It goes without saying that one of the two was a child of Black Caribbean heritage. The borough had tried to look into the reasons for why this particular group are disproportionately affected, but I have to report that the research being conducted was so light touch and void of attempting to address the huge complexities and anomalies that I resented even being asked to take part.

I recall asking questions like, 'Have you looked into the good examples? Have you considered how those others (successful ones) are not represented in the statistics?' They had not and I could feel my frustration building up. In my seat at the table, I need to do more, I need to accomplish and contribute more but it cannot happen by me alone. For this reason, I am reticent to participate in piecemeal initiatives supposedly to address the overrepresentation of students of Black or brown heritage in the exclusion statistics. I am on a mission to change this, one child at a time. It is, of course, challenging as you juggle various priorities, some needing addressing immediately as they will have a greater impact on the entire mass and not just on the 'only 26%' of your school population of Black or brown heritage.

I did a term of what many would term 'normal headship'. And then, like an unannounced visitor, along came the Covid-19 pandemic and, with it, new words. Some I had used in different contexts – like 'lockdown', a procedure I led as Safeguarding Lead as part of a drill like the fire drill – and others I had never even heard of before like 'furlough'. Covid-19 just sat in my school's living room and gate-crashed, reducing all my plans to ink on paper and imposing a mighty pause to my progress. It was such an intrusion.

I can honestly say that being the Designated Safeguarding Lead was probably one of the best roles I had that prepared me for headship. Talk about dealing with the 'unprecedented', that overused word since 2019! Anything can come at you from child abuse stories to missing children through to concerns about staff members and even as far-fetched as dealing with a gun shoot-out in a local supermarket and ensuring the safety of your older students who are commuting between sites, at the same time as locking down the school.

As a headteacher, intrusions and 'unprecedented' issues arise continuously and come at you from all angles. But no living headteacher had ever dealt with leading a school through a pandemic.

I completely understand the sense of urgency we have as headteachers and the wish, the passion and the desire to see the differences that we want to see. When I decided to do a 'three-questions' meeting with every member of staff, I had pledged that I would do this, and I began this right from the start of the very first set of 100 days. I had timed it so that by the end of that academic year I would have had a quality 15 minutes with every member of staff appointed at my school. It started off great. It was my audit of the school.

Frankly, it meant that I also opened myself up to hearing some hard and harsh words. I always started each meeting explaining the context, explaining that this was a completely confidential meeting, that the only readers of the notes I was taking would be myself, and that they had 15 minutes of quality time with me where I wanted them to be completely candid, open and honest, without fear of any questioning, monitoring, accountability, or any comeback.

Each individual always started off with being a little bit guarded, but by the end of the 15 minutes, when time was up, I couldn't shut them up. Most were in full swing and full flow and we often went on a little longer. I gained so much from these conversations.

My three-questions flow was completely interrupted by the coronavirus pandemic, with the several periods of school closure. It slowed down the progress through my to-do list, it stopped me learning the names of all 1,200 students I had set myself the target of achieving. I had come from a school with almost 1,700 students and I damn near knew every single child by first name. Remember what I said earlier, this was important. Every child is an individual who deserves you to at least know their name. I was intentional about learning the names of my new 'babies'. The gaps caused by school closures made this impossible in my potentially unrealistic time frame, especially by not being in the classroom regularly anymore. I might have learnt 30 new names in a week, one minute, and the next I was sending that group home for isolation.

Rapidly, due to my love of technology and all things on a computer screen, we moved our school to 'the cloud' and embraced at breakneck speed the transition to remote learning.

In the end, after precisely two years and one month to the day … I completed my set target of meeting with every one of the 168 members of staff for the three-questions meeting. It was worth it; it was worth every word that was spoken in those meetings. Never mind getting to know each person on an individual basis, what made them tick, what made them passionate, what their aspirations were, in some cases the history of where they stood, how they had joined the school, but certainly the answers to the following three questions were the prize-winners:

1. What is the one thing that you love about the school and, with a new head, you were thinking this must stay and never change?
2. What is the one thing that has been bugging you that you feel with a new head there is now an opportunity to change or could be different?
3. What are your expectations of me as the headteacher?

On many occasions, staff would decorate what they said initially and then their authentic selves would show up and take over and I would be exposed to all manner of insights into different areas of the school. It was wonderful. I was able to embrace and take on the bad, even smile and sometimes already give myself a pat on the back, with comments that highlighted changes that had recently been observed that they approved of or admired.

Depending on my mood and the events of my day, sometimes it was also hard and difficult to hear some of the truths.

As Jim Collins (2001) says to confront the brutal facts, I did that when I heard things related to student behaviour, for example, a much-needed tightening up of the system or a necessity to introduce new rules and new procedures, comments about staff or student wellbeing. Usually, I agreed with the thoughts, realising how perceptive the staff were, as they were things I was already thinking about. What made it difficult was the fact that I knew that these were the truths, and it meant that I would need in some way, shape or form to address these – the staff were counting on me being able to and I wanted to be sure I would and was equipped to do so.

The problem with me was I wanted to address everything all at once. I'm quite impatient, so like them, I wanted to see behaviour suddenly, magically be improved so that people would talk about seeing and feeling the difference. I wanted to make sure that homework was completely in line with expectations, to see that every teacher was consistently giving and marking homework set and at the highest standard and submitted at the best quality. I wanted to see that every child was getting a sense of satisfaction and making good progress. My nerves were constantly on edge between necessity, excitement and urgency.

The brutal fact was that this was a new part of my journey. I was in a different form of transportation and I needed to persevere and say to myself that I would tackle one priority at a time. 'Put first things first', as Stephen Covey (1989) states – the idea that keeping the main thing, the main thing, was essential.

The key tools to do this would need to be the school improvement plan, communication via regular staff touch-base meetings, but in the absence of whole staff briefings. Due to the pandemic, the challenge of arriving at consistent practice with key messages to all staff all the time regularly was definitely prevalent.

Often, I had to have some quiet words with myself and give myself reality checks about what was reasonable to achieve, what I needed to prioritise and what I needed to address. Other times, thankfully, my deputy heads did this for me in their own ways. Importantly, it was recognising the worth and the value of my senior leadership team, to recognise when I needed to unpick my frustrations, to know exactly what my vision was for the school and to be on the same path to get there, that was key.

My NPQH coach had transitioned to being a valuable individual from yesteryear. I had moved on to having a 'headteacher' coach. This coach throughout all of this period of 'newness' was indispensable. And I am so grateful for his time and his frankness.

It was great to be able to have a coach who understood me and the job at hand. It was great to be able to have a coach who didn't worry about the length of time we spent in conversation, who understood that sometimes a very quick phone call, cutting to the chase and getting into the heart of the problem so we could get to a solution, didn't mean that either one of us was being rude, abrupt or disregarding the other. We didn't always flounder about with niceties and greetings. Time was of the essence if I called him to deal with a pertinent behaviour issue, parental concern or someone threatening the school community. A mutual understanding here was vital, and our relationship worked.

There was an understanding of mutual respect regarding our precious time and the importance of it. His input and insight in helping me navigate the early days of headship were more than crucial. For any aspirant heads reading this, one simple advice – get a coach ... or two!

Some people argue that if you have too many coaches you may seek too much counsel. However, I found that I was able to seek counsel from the different voices and then discern what resonated with me and what aligned with my values and my authentic self. Whatever made my gut relax, aligned with my values and would help me make decisions. Sometimes it was the counsel of the former coach, other times it was my CEO, other times it was my fellow headteachers or even the voice of my husband on occasion who acted as an exemplary coach and counsel.

Lucky is putting it mildly when it came to me landing this job in a borough where there was already an inbuilt peer coaching capacity. The ability to bounce things off another head is invaluable and could not have been more so than at a time when I was new to headship and striving to lead my school, 1,200 students (and their parents) and 168 staff through a school year in a pandemic. It was relentless. It was so tough.

The blog I created when I began my journey to headship in 2013 had not seen me for the last two years. I didn't feel the need to record my reflections in it, rather enjoying the reflections of others for a time.

Occasions of sending 'bubbles' home at a moment's notice, making several decisions and plans without knowing what changes were around the corner, being unable to give concrete decisions for things and, of course, the dreaded management of any horrible, harrowing or sad issues that arose drove me to momentary insomnia at times. I faced sickness, disputes, union concerns, parent pushbacks to some of our measures, managing the emotions of the entire school community as they handled their distrust of government actions very badly, or even as we heard of their many bereavements. Following the ups and downs of some sleepless nights or extremely early mornings, I was driven to write this poetic reflection which stayed in my drafts until I began to write this book:

> Coronavirus, you are a double-edged sword.
> You are a pain and a headache on the one hand.
> You cause so much literal pain and grief and sadness.
> You strip humans of hope and fill them with despair. You create the life of a headteacher to go into an automated machine that needs to create and churn out optimism, all the while in the midst of her own uncertainty, doubt and second-guessing.
>
> But ...
> Covid-19, you also present freedom, time and newness.
> The freedom and space to be with the ones we love, given the choice.
> The freedom to design our days from start to finish and not keep on the racetrack.
>
> The freedom to use up the time, to take up new hobbies, or ones we left years ago and never thought we would rekindle.
> The time to sit and meditate and the time to take on new skills if we decide we want a new way of doing things, thinking things, experiencing things.
> If we really want to, Covid-19, we can use you to the benefit of us all and make this world a better place.

This government, well, what can we say?
After having read an article clearly stating that the guardians of the nation's children, in other words, us headteachers, have been the real policy creators and drivers without there being real policymakers, we have taken the bull by the horns, considered the answers before they asked us the questions:

How? When? Where? Will we learn, read, play, study, and even eat? Free school meals for us was never an afterthought but the first.
Safeguarding is like an embedded chip, we are continuously programmed to start at that point and look at life for anyone affected so we can plan purposefully, as best we can using our best resources, our staff, to help us.
Oh, Coronavirus and Covid-19, Corona – Virus – starting in 2019 is the breakdown.

It really does not matter what your name is.

You will not remain on roll in our register, only as an afterthought, a 'remember when' period and a distant but happily remembered time of when headteachers were working in solidarity towards a common goal for a common enemy with the government officials closely following behind, not quite sure what to do ... our leaders, being led by the true leaders.

The long-time unspoken heroes – many of whom are now in the forefront of the minds of everyone – the NHS workers, filled with ... oh yes, all those we want to send back to where they come from, mainly the BAME workers who are saving lives but also giving up their lives.

It sounds like a war out there!
The teachers and all the support staff workers who brave their journeys in, to be with those vulnerable ones and ensure that the schools provide a safety hub for all as required.

The newness of words like 'furlough' and 'PPE'

Lockdown
Exams cancelled
Vulnerable
Staff safety
Online community – digital world came alive
Policy vacuum
Social service shirking

PPE
Social distancing – physical distancing
Loss, tragedy …

Confidence, hope,
… Optimism

What a year. Not only did I manage to endure a year filled with uncertainties and survive the dreaded virus myself, but I avoided excluding the eight Year 11 boys who had clearly lost the plot and were causing absolute mayhem for their new head and her team.

One deputy keeping me up to date with minute-by-minute detail of the escapades of those high-profile Year 11 boys – eight of whom finally jumped our fence, making a mockery of our sheer exhaustion. I told my deputy head I wanted to wait, wait until we knew what was happening with schools. The boys had been involved in all sorts of shenanigans, including escaping the school, being anti-social and just insolence. It happens every year if students are not well-trained in readiness for exams. I call it a case of what I have named 'Examitis'. This is when a few students, so close to their final days in the year of their exams (Key Stage 4), just lose it. It becomes, in my book, an affliction, and our challenge is to save them from themselves and make them get to the very end. They manifest it in different ways but this group were just taking the biscuit, as they say.

From my bed, instead of relaxing, I was emailing letters left, right and centre, and directing the next steps, between paracetamol and coconut water. The only things I could keep down. I could not believe this was me. The head, off sick? No way! I kept thinking: 'Sick? I can't be sick, there is no time for that.' Call it 'new head syndrome' but a sense of guilt, I admit, also wove its way into my head.

My deputies were phenomenal. The word team came into true effect. I am convinced it was Covid-19 but back then in March 2020 there were no tests, and no one could confirm anything.

Eventually, it was announced. Schools were going to be closed. There was no need to exclude the band of merry men in Year 11. Phew!

I will say it again. The important thing was to know my values and know what aligned and you would know when it didn't sit right with you because it wouldn't leave for ages. Once I had wrestled with the different viewpoints and ideas and come to a verdict, I would always know when I was comfortable with my decision and I would sleep like a baby at night-time.

On the odd occasion it did bother me, it meant I needed to have a further conversation with myself or think about what the outcomes would be or sometimes just wait. That is not always easy to do.

Being an individual who admittedly suffers from the perfection addiction, one of the defaults is always trying to get the perfect answer and please everyone. But the ability to realise that this isn't always possible means that you can quickly bounce back and regulate yourself, make a decision, sit with it but be prepared for any fallout by having the support of others ready.

Preparedness is key.

16. A Seat at the Table

'The fear of taking off the armour is universal.'

(Brené Brown, 2018)

'Black children have emotions. Black children cry. I find your level of empathy insipid.' (An upset parent)

This was the extract from an email from a Black mother, looking out for her daughter. I came home that evening and could think of nothing else but how I would make this situation better. How would I go about this meeting? What would I need to do to prepare? How might the mother react? How could I lead the meeting effectively with the desired outcome but not undermine my colleague? The words used in the email were so strong and attacking. I was lost on how I could undo the damage and yet conscious of my reputation also being on the line.

You see, being Black and being in a prominent position comes with a huge responsibility. I felt as though I had the issues of the entire Black population on my shoulders and the burden of getting it right for them will almost certainly impact me. If you are white, you don't have to worry about 'your people' and how damaging it will be. You see yourself as you are, and nothing and no one will change the perception of you. But as a Black woman, also from the 'ends', it mattered to me. It mattered that I would keep my integrity intact. It mattered that I would not be seen to be appeasing to placate only my colleagues and suffer the consequence of my reputation being slandered as someone who did not have the interests of the Black community at heart. Potentially, being called a 'fake' or, worse, a 'coconut'.

Nothing could be further from the truth. I felt that my position meant that I had the opportunity to let this mother, and many like her, be heard. The mother whose daughter had made a bee-line for me on my very first visit to the school and proceeded to do her 30-second 'elevator speech'. 'Hello, Miss. My name is Sky. Are you going to be our new headteacher? I am so happy to meet you. I am really keen on drama and I intend to go to the BRIT School, Miss. Anyway, I just wanted to come over and introduce myself to you.'

Sky needed no introduction. And I was quickly apprised that she had the time to accost me, because she was out of lessons instead of being in them. It mattered. That right there was a show of why visibility is important. Why representation matters and why we cannot refute the claims that race does play a role in the education of our young people. A sense of identity and belonging is important. There is a place for the phrase 'you cannot be what you cannot see', although I agree that you can also find inspiration in those who are different to us as well.

In her mother's email, I could feel the built-up tension of many years of possible difficulty; she referred to it as 'oppression'. Not just of her but of Black people in general. I could sense from the contents that she wanted to recount her condensed version of the whole Black history to the reader in an email. I could feel her fear and frustration, but I could also sense something else. I learnt later that what I sensed was simply a mother, desperate for a break, finding life hard and navigating the challenges. It's a very complex situation. Not only would ruining my reputation be harmful to me; more importantly, it would harm the reputation of my beautiful school. A school you could not describe as anything other than diverse, with an array of children working hard towards their unknown futures.

Image: iStock.com/monkeybusinessimages

What many wouldn't know is how I played and replayed the different permutations of the conversation that was to be and how I would respond in every situation. I did have a goal and I knew I probably would give some of myself away in the conversation as it could help. It was time to take off some of the armour. The questions were: what parts of me? how much? and when? In my world the stakes are high.

Act too officious and I could lose this parent forever and have a very offended child to contain for the remainder of her time with us. Act too friendly and I would be open to all sorts of unnecessary contact, communication and even some liberty-taking, potentially. The internal struggle between living according to one's own values and dealing with my own and others' emotional baggage was evident.

I needed to stick to my values. What were they? I remembered: respect, integrity, fairness, joy and happiness, support and encouragement, peace, understanding and excellence. All whilst being a very visible leader.

I had to do this right. I had a seat at the table. If not me, then who?

Several emotive parent meetings later and admittedly with some trial and error, I think we had some success. I believe I also achieved this with damage limitation to my school – a school recognised by some in the community as not always meeting the needs of particular communities (and by that I mean Black families) and the staff within it as well. The student made it, albeit with additional challenges along the way and right up to her final day's presence at the school, but she achieved a good set of GCSEs, allowing her to move on. I do hope she has gone on to pursue her dreams, with success. I also hope her memories and the support received will not go amiss and have gone some way to disintegrate the prior judgements held about the school.

This for me is part of my role, to instil a sense of hope and trust in an education system that is not always deemed fair or accessible to all.

17. 2020 Vision? An Unprecedented Year

'Daring leadership is leading from heart, not hurt '

(Brené Brown, 2018)

Moving into year two of my headship was an awesome feeling and I have tried to be, as Maya Angelou entitles her poem, a Phenomenal Woman. The Google women's empowerment initiative slogan reads '#I am remarkable' (Google, 2021) and I have also tried to maintain that mantra.

No longer at the starting blocks, I felt, as the mafia said, 'made' – when you have withstood the trials and not been moved and are fully initiated. A quick search on Wikipedia will inform you that, 'In the American and Sicilian Mafia, a "made man" is a fully initiated member of the Mafia' (Wikipedia, n.d.). I was fully initiated into headship of a different kind and had sort of completed one academic year cycle.

The school year is the same every year, but it is punctuated with exciting events and no two days are ever the same. Take a look at the events of this particular week, for example, which I gave subheadings to:

Monday – 'The gravedigger'

Tuesday – 'Covid-19 case 2'

Wednesday – 'The escapee and the fence jumper'

Thursday – 'Covid-19 case 3'

Friday – I cried, so what?

Monday – 'The gravedigger'

Simon had taken the day off work. He had argued with my PA at the time that he did not want it to count as a day off work as he had felt better by the afternoon and then decided to do other things. Other things? With public money? I don't think so. It turns out that he clearly wanted to have the day at home. It makes you wonder what drives people's motives. I had summoned him to my office, but he had not come. I got my PA to do the meeting with him instead and find out the details of where he was on that day in March. Then we were hit by the lockdown and I decided that it was better to focus on the wider school community and the more critical scenarios – you know, things like bereavement, depression of certain individuals and real genuine heartfelt cases of others in need amongst my staff, rather than spend time on one individual who had not cared to follow, or even recognise that the school has, procedures.

We left it for the time being. April came and went. May, June, July and then August. But I was not going to let this slip. We had resumed in full in September and I had asked my PA to remind me to follow this up. My PA was made to feel she had in some way been prejudiced towards this colleague in the meeting I had instructed to investigate. I eventually got my later-appointed PA to call Simon to a meeting at the given time to be held in my office. He came. I told him that I only deal in honesty, that he had seen how I operate now for a year and that I wear my heart on my sleeve and like people to be honest also with me. I asked where he was on that day in March.

After going around the houses he explained his story. Something about a sick child and then his own tummy upset or something. I asked why he had not simply followed the leave of absence policy and he said he did not know about it. After four years in the establishment, he did not know. Well, bully for you, previous SLT, clearly your leadership sucked if this colleague was not informed about your well-established procedures that the other 167 members of staff know of and use on a regular basis!

I paused. I let him speak. I let him dig the rest of the grave his wife had begun to dig for him. The wife, who reached the point that she felt the need to email the school to ask that I call her to discuss things before speaking to Simon. Let's just say thoughts of a domineering domestic situation came to my mind. After a while, I asked, 'So didn't you attend an interview?'

Simon's face twitched. I could feel the floor opening up for him. He grew pale and stared beyond me. His mouth was half ajar. His secret was out and he knew it. I then asked simply, 'Do you know how I know you were not ill but going for an interview?' Simon turned sheepishly, and looked at me wide-eyed.

'The headteacher of the school you went to called me. The headteacher explained to me you had been for an interview and that the behaviour of your wife when she had called the school made it very uncomfortable and the headteacher felt she had to let me know.'

Silence.

You could hear a pin drop. I have to be honest, I had an internal smirk on my face behind the poker one. I felt like saying 'Gotcha!' But, of course, I did not. I simply let Simon lie in the grave he had dug and gasp for air.

Then I launched in and explained why he had not upheld the seven principles of public life, honesty being one, and that I was terribly disappointed and would consider my next steps. I am not one to do this normally, but I wanted him to sweat a bit. I believe with some it is the only way to learn, once you feel the deep shit you are in for a while. The same way a child may do when caught out, I suppose.

Meanwhile, I already had my 'strong management advice' letter written in draft, ready to proof and click 'send'. I also told him that I did not employ his wife and that he needed to go home and have a conversation with her.

Tuesday – Covid-19 case 2

In the morning, I had spoken with my SLT about the fear of having a positive Covid-19 case amongst our Year 11 students and the possibility of sending them home. What a nightmare that would be.

We had a lovely evening with our new Year 7 parents' meeting with their children's form tutors that was due to end at 6:30 p.m. It was meant to be home-time. Guess what? Home-time for those present was extended by at least two more hours due to a positive Covid-19 case amongst Year 11 and all the track and trace that followed.

The problem was, we had been told via a phone call from a mother who had by chance had her child tested, as he was in hospital for other things. One thing that struck me was that he had also had diarrhoea which I felt was beginning to rear its head amongst some students, and my instinct was telling me this was an unrecognised Covid-19 symptom.

By 7:30 p.m., we were still there, making calls to staff, gathering evidence and tracking and tracing. I had left my beloved hubby outside waiting to collect me since 6:30 p.m., had got caught up in it all, and 45 minutes later, I was jolted into this realisation as my phone rang with his name on the screen. I left immediately, letting my colleagues know I would have the laptop out and be at home sorting out the letters in ten minutes. After all, it was after 7:30 p.m. – most of the admin staff were at home!

I managed to write the letters to the 25 students we identified that day, personally addressed to the students. I sent them to the single admin staff member left who had graciously waited in order to email them to the parents, only to be met in the morning with a barrage of frantic parental phone calls, fielded by my excellent staff responding to ridiculous questions, such as 'Is my child to stay home as there is a case of the virus?'

It's easy to respond, 'Duh, no, if they were, we would have told you, stupid!' but of course, that is out of the question and, actually, you can't blame them. No one knew what to think and believe and the air was filled with the government's lack of clarity and therefore indecision. So questions and assumptions were the order of the day and schools had become the haven for all the answers and remedies of society's problems, raising the nation's children and buffering the government from the wrath of parental uncertainty. It was the last straw when I got the letter from a parent accusing the school of not being on the front foot and being able to 'forward plan'. I felt incensed and so angry. I was by then also very tired.

Dear husband helped me see it was one parent only, in the grand scheme of things. He certainly has a place in my life as the one who calms me down and helps me regain perspective. I was greatly reassured on speaking to a fellow head about my decision who told me she had dealt with six cases whilst I was in a stir about only two.

Wednesday – 'The escapee and the fence jumper'

I was looking forward to eating my home-cooked lunch. Today's was my amazing salad and turkey slices. Believe me, in my book this was wonderful. Getting to eat it was going to make it amazing. I would just make my way back to my office after my wonderful visits to lessons which I had really enjoyed. The sky was still blue and there was a glimmer of sunshine too in the autumn airspace.

Panting and puffing, the cover supervisor tried to let me know he had seen one of our students make a run for it and escaping. He had jumped over the back gate. He managed to give a description. Blue shirt – that narrows it down, as Year 11 wear black and white – short with dark hair. Great. Did anyone know who he was? No. Did the staff sitting in the car park with the gates wide open who should really be held to account for the escape act see him and seem able to apprehend him or inform adequately? No. Not so great then. So there it was. Right in the middle of a normal-ish day, I had a serious safeguarding issue with an unknown boy wandering outside the safety of the school and no one knew a damn thing. Suddenly the sky turned grey. My exquisite and lovingly made lunch would once again have to wait.

I walked briskly to the other end of our building, the bus stop end. I had the skill of anticipation.

The student had sprinted away from the staff member, and when he arrived at the bus stop side of the school perimeter, he jumped over our very high fence to the main road, about to make a run for it, and landed right in front of … me. Caught red-handed is an understatement. But in the mind of a 14-year-old boy, he believes he is wearing an invisible cloak. Isn't that normal for everyone?

In my Mrs Manderson way, I marched him back into the school after making him complete my bus stop duty with me, and asked a member of staff to call home to inform and send the child safely home with a time stamp.

I swiftly went to the curriculum meeting we had in store. The next thing I knew, I was being told there was a distraught mother in reception as her child had not arrived home – guess who? Yes, the fence jumper himself. I was told the Safeguarding Lead was dealing with it and was sending the parent home with a call to the police.

Those of us in the education game immediately know what must have been going on. For those not in our sinister mindset, let me give you an indication. He jumps over the fence, gets caught by the headteacher, and the parent is called. Next stop is not home but a faraway park, for fear of what may be more terrifying than being caught by the headteacher. See what I mean? In other words, could it be that he was fearful of an enraged parent, who could maybe even inflict violence towards him, so that he avoided going home? I called the home to check whether he had turned up. There was no answer. I persevered until minutes to 7 p.m. before giving up trying to get hold of the parent to triple-check the status of the whereabouts of the child, even after my DHT had already called twice. I resigned myself to the fact that my DHT had made contact and spoken to a parent and had told them to go to the police if needed.

Only then did I go home.

That night, like a living unwanted nightmare, both incidents stayed on my mind. What would I be faced with in the morning this time?

Thursday – 'Covid-19 case 3'

You could not make this up. Not one but now two cases in the same year group but this time we were not so lucky as the student had been happily mingling with her peers for three days! By the time we were done, I had sent home another 46 students, making it a grand total of 71 Year 11 students needing to self-isolate out of the cohort of 210.

I had the experience of watching myself grow and develop better decision-making as I paused and reflected on what I needed to do. Should I send home the whole year group? Maybe not, but cover things in my letter. In between the crazy running up and down of track and trace, locating and serving letters to all students, calling parents and ensuring that we were adhering to guidelines, I still managed to participate and give my talk at the virtual London Mayor's Office event as part of the Look Like Me Book Challenge, created by Winsome Duncan with 30 budding authors of Black and ethnic minority heritage on the Microsoft Teams video conference.

It acted as a break, surprisingly, and I left the conference feeling more clear-headed and decisive than I had been prior to it. As they say, a change is as good as a rest and it really was in this case.

I had an out-of-body experience as I watched myself in action and surprised myself by the calm and control I was exuding. Only the night before, dear husband had highlighted to me a great leadership lesson as we watched *The Crown* (Morgan, 2019). I should correct that to say as 'he' watched *The Crown* and I crashed out on the sofa beside him.

It was episode three of season 3. In the wake of her visit to the Welsh mining town of **Aberfan** that had suffered the loss of 144 of its citizens, 116 of them children, when a slag pit of coal ash buried part of the village, the Queen reflected. Prime Minister (PM) Harold Wilson visited immediately, but the Queen waited a week, and in retrospect, she realised that she had been wrong.

In the episode, the Queen shares her lack of empathy and emotion with ex-PM Harold Wilson who responds by enlightening her with the acts of leadership that he recognises makes others feel a sense of reassurance. The lesson was that leaders are there to make others feel calm and reassured, not to be in a flap. Well, he puts it better than me by saying of leaders, 'our job is to calm more crises than we create' and 'no one needs hysteria from a Head of State'. I take out 'of state' and replace it with 'teacher'. He was absolutely spot on.

Dear husband said he watched this part and smiled, as he looked over at Ertha Hooks High school's leader, mouth wide open, sprawled out on the bed, snoring her head off, and he smiled and thought, 'Yes, she does this at work – if only they could see her now: here is Ertha Hooks High school's leader'.

I absolutely love my job, my vocation, my mission. Being a headteacher is truly, I feel, one of the best jobs in the world. The coronavirus pandemic was an unbelievably unprecedented event. No one could ever have seen that coming and it surely would have done me in if I did not feel so wedded to my profession and believe in being a champion for the children.

I have carefully selected a network of individuals and engage in 'give and take'. It's good for the soul and definitely needed when the going gets tough in headship. Joining a school afresh brings new challenges. There are so many ups and downs, unexpected events and deadlines to meet. The weight of managing everyone's expectations.

But I'm not alone. The beauty of being a new head who knows other headteachers is that you can share and see who comes out best for the worst as you can see from one WhatsApp exchange below, demonstrating the camaraderie which ensued following a pandemic week of sheer madness:

Me:
These last two weeks:
3 grievances to conclude,
1 potential parent complaint
Parent and new staff member altercation
(Not just the kids!)
Reopening stresses with timetable
Angry parent and annoying advocate thinking we can pay for private education!

I could go on but my biggest challenge all year has been getting through this week. Imagine

Bring on Friday 4pm!

Nadege:
Yep this week has been tough. I've had parental complaints and members of staff receiving aggressive and threatening emails with demands to see me directly!

Monica:

OK so we're playing new head top trumps hey? One staff disciplinary investigation, senior leader signed off sick, boiler broke, and we had a flood and FGB went on to 8.45pm tonight after I started work at 4am this morning. And my damn reopening letter is still not done! Check out our pension statements ladies??! 🙈🙉🙊

Nadege:
Conclusion:
OK you win Monica! it's certainly been in at the deep end!! If it's any consolation I've only sent a holding letter with a more detailed one to follow towards the end of the summer.

Me:
Omg
I don't feel alone anymore!!!!!! This is great we'll have some energy to go on! There's definitely a pink gin with my name on it tomorrow night 🍸chin, chin! Ladies 😊nearly there!!

Thanks Nadege and Monica.

Senior leader signed off! Oh dear, guess we are all human. I was up till 4 am Saturday doing risk assessment so I know the feeling! Still haven't caught up on sleep.

Letter sent today but risk assessment still to tidy!

Madness.

Friday – I cried, so what?

There have been many times where I recognise that crying is not a sign of weakness. In the midst of the George Floyd tragedy, I wrote a poem called 'I Cried'. In that poem, I wrote about my sense of being a parent of Black boys in the United Kingdom; although not in the equivalent scenario as being in the United States, the killing of George Floyd pulled on the heartstrings of many mothers of Black males, regardless of their age and their location, and I was one of them. It was a conversation that needed to be had and I recognise that I am a person who is prone to cry.

So yes, there have been occasions where I recognised that crying is not a sign of weakness. Damn, many a time I have quoted those words to someone else.

However, I will admit that concurrently I view it as a weakness to myself. Case in point – on Friday 13 November 2020, yes Friday the 13th, once again, I cried. But this time it was at the fact that I was going to deliver some news to approximately 170 children aged 15 approaching 16, about the fact that they would now be sent home for two weeks of remote learning. Just before their mock examinations were to begin.

As I walked past the Year 11 students who lined up gradually in the playground, I heard a lovely sound. The sound of a young man greeting me. 'Hi, Miss,' he said, and another, 'Hey, Mrs Manderson, how are you?' It was so beautiful, and I thought to myself, if only they knew the news I was about to deliver to them. Poor things. Having had to contend with the high tensions and exhausting track and trace process resulting from three confirmed positive cases of coronavirus amongst students in that year group earlier this week, which had wiped out the already 50 missing students from the cohort, I was on my knees and felt emotionally drained.

We had been on our feet or constantly on the computers, physically or mentally rushing around all week, and I say 'we' because the amount of people (and energy) it took to organise sending out one letter to parents just to let them know the facts was colossal.

My team and I were working hard all around this pandemic, yet the repercussions in schools were immense and with no additional support or funding. Still, the accountability remained very high. Every head had to do right by everybody.

As I was about to deliver the message to Year 11 to send them home, for a flash moment, I had a strong surge of thought to myself:

> *I have a son in Year 11 and how would I feel if he had to be sent home for two weeks, knowing that he would be put at a disadvantage to many of his peers around the country and the impact on the results that they are about to receive, not just for now but for his future? A very uncertain future. But these results could give them a grounding, some certainty in a world of uncertainty – it's simply not fair.*

And it suddenly overwhelmed me.

All of a sudden, I felt my face contort. 'Oh shit, I'm about to cry, I really am about to cry and I can't stop it,' I heard my inner voice say. I looked up and saw one of my assistant heads who said those exact three words that people ask which make it all the worse, 'Are you okay?', and that was it.

The tears began to flood out and as I turned around, flustered, fighting to find a way out of my situation, I felt my ex-PA catching me and saying, 'Come on, this way', and quickly putting her arm around me and ushering me in the direction of the stairs I had clearly lost sight of.

We disappeared into the building, as slick as oil seeping through a gap.

I had done the unthinkable. I had finally submitted to something I had dreaded until it had actually happened today. I wanted to avoid crying. I had managed to so far, following the turbulent first year, the trying Year 11s, the demanding parents, the shocking and sometimes very distressing news of staff or their family or friends, the Covid-19 cases, the union demands, the numerous student fights I had had the pleasure of breaking up or dealing with, the permanent exclusions and all else that had happened.

The truth is I was emotionally spent. My head was overfull with decisions and thoughts and I had been on autopilot. As Viv Grant states in her book *Staying A Head* (2014):

> When you are working in a school, engaging every day with children and their families, teachers, support staff, governors and many other adults, you know that you spend as much, if not more, energy meeting the emotional needs of others. As a result, you end up carrying a huge emotional debt and become increasingly emotionally overdrawn, with no readily identifiable means for bringing your emotional account back into credit.

At least I had not cried at all in my first year but at the beginning of my second year. However, I had cried in front of staff. It didn't matter that it was only two, it was in front of staff, although at least not in front of students, or at least that's what I thought.

Fortunately, I was able to pull myself together, behind the security and safety of another colleague, and use up all the energy I could muster to breathe deeply and compose myself. I opened my eyes wide in an effort to evaporate the tears speedily and I fanned my eyes with my hands, hoping to lessen the redness. We looked at each other and I whispered, 'I'll be okay', then we shared a smile. After a very brief but momentous pause, I braced myself and calmly and coolly strolled outside, sauntered down the steps, made that intense walk to the children in their lines and proceeded to address my wonderful students with a strong voice.

There were particular students on my mind, and I worried about the consequences of this decision for each of them. Would this return Jason, the six-foot-five student we had taken in from the Pupil Referral Unit, to the streets? Jason, previously permanently excluded from another school for bringing a knife into the school, but who had been a reformed and shining character in the short time with us? Would this give him the get-out clause to return once more to the streets? Would I once again be informed by our local police he had been arrested with drugs and armour in a flat? I went up to him before he left his line and he looked me dead in my reddened eyes. I didn't care. I asked him, 'Will you be okay?'

Jason gave me his charming slow smile and nodded, silently. As he left, he lifted up his hood on his black puffer and made his way.

The student with special educational needs, Marcus, whose face became filled with dread at the prospect of not receiving support whilst he would be at home – how could we ease this period of time for him and let him know he would be okay? I asked the head of year to pull him to the side and do a quick welfare check. Did he have all the equipment he needed? Did he have a place to sit and read comfortably? What about the internet, was everything working? Did he know how to contact the school? Did he remember the members of the safeguarding and the special educational needs team he could call on? He was shaking following the announcement. By the time we had finished speaking with him, his nerves were calmed, and he was smiling, making his way out of the gate with the Special Needs Coordinator (SENCo) right behind him.

What about the self-harmer and school-refuser, Selma, who we had tirelessly worked with to get into school regularly – would she just lose hope? My Safeguarding Lead didn't even look in my direction following the announcement. She needed no authorisation. It was a given. Our school would always be there for the vulnerable even if, at this point, they were being sent home. She knew exactly which students to see and speak to before they left the site. All was in hand.

All of them were children of ethnic heritage. It was interesting to observe their heightened levels of anxiety compared to some others, maybe some even more deprived financially than them. But there was something else that made them feel less secure. It was difficult to put your finger on it.

My poor Year 11. School, the safe haven for many, would be unavailable to them for at least two more weeks at such a critical time.

I knew my children knew that I was doing right by them. They had felt my deep-rooted passion and trusted me. It rang through as they bid me farewell with 'Bye, Miss', and 'See you online, Miss' as they left, assured that their headteacher and staff would continue to look after them, even if remotely.

That experience has taught me that,

> To be a school leader, whether as a Headteacher or in another role, is to be human. (Grant, 2014)

My job in the past two years has been to improve outcomes for children and increase their life chances, literally, by improving the conditions for teaching and learning, and that's a massive job. You don't do that with just one small project or single-handedly. You do that through monitoring and support, through training, coaching, mentoring, hard work, collegiality, being persistent in working with and through others, leading and being led and everything in between.

I love it. I thrive on it.

I only wish there were more like me, who look like me, doing this for children who look like them. I can remember speaking to a young teacher who expressed her fear of moving into senior leadership and her fascination with being a headteacher. She had said she would not even have thought of going into middle leadership had she not met and spoken with me. I explained to her why she needed to be representative and how rewarding it could be.

To those of you who represent an ethnic 'minority', especially you if you are reading this book, please do not shy away from leadership. You must strive towards it.

> Leadership is not the private reserve of a few charismatic men and women. It is a process that ordinary people use when they are bringing forth the best in themselves and others. (Harris 2007 as cited in Grant 2014).

We need you.

The future generations need you.

Epilogue

In the UK, the terms 'Black boys' and 'exclusions' have been heard all too often within the same sentence. How I wish that my position meant I could genuinely create change. Change is required. It is urgent. There are far too many iterations of this overrepresentation of Black students, especially boys, in negative ways. I can't do it alone, and schools cannot be the sole solution.

Becoming a headteacher is an amazing accomplishment. I am the mother of 1,200 kids! That's what I think every day. I literally want to know that we are doing everything we can for them. In front of me during every assembly could be a future lawyer, doctor, supermarket manager or worker or even Prime Minister – who knows? Even if they do have to work 11 times harder. I have had one student promise me she will become Britain's first Black and female Prime Minister. Currently aged 15, so let's see what happens around 20 years from now.

This book has been about my journey. My thoughts and feelings are exposed to offer camaraderie to anyone else going through alone some of the emotions I have had, especially when considering the next steps in a career. It is also a call to the top guns in this country to think about school leaders, why we have so very few from Black and other ethnic groups, but also to have some consideration for all the historic experiences they come with when they get there. Think about the representation in our schools and think about whether or not there is a need to address the ills of our society – namely, disadvantage and prejudices that create an invisible barrier to potentially thousands of other competent and magical leaders in schools.

It is a call to action to get these ridiculous statistics to a better level, not in 20 years, but now. By addressing societal influences, media messages and negative rhetoric, we should be able to influence change. Not by the means of a small amount of money being thrown at a meaningless project which looks at the stories of ten out of thousands of Black boys who have been excluded, for example. As if this will be the magic wand!

I wish I had the answers.

There are several out there like me. There are many out there who could someday become what I have become. Some of them might even sit in your assemblies!

What a world it will be if progression in the education domain can be reached by anyone who chooses to go up this path. However, it will take allies and champions to encourage individuals from an early age. We cannot expect current heads to magic future leaders from ethnic backgrounds if there is no field to draw upon. But we should expect governing bodies of schools to be both reflective of their populations, diverse enough to represent different voices, and to also see the potential in the right candidate, irrespective of their ethnicity.

Social media groups like #Blackteachersofinstagram, Blackteachersconnect and Blackteachers_educate exist because there is a need to gather solidarity amongst a group who know how important it is to strive for change. They exist to share knowledge, expertise and experience across the diaspora. Social media makes evolution easier to accomplish across the seas.

The school year never changes. In the UK, we start afresh in September each new academic year, we have the half terms and the larger holidays at Christmas and Easter and then, as the French say, 'les grandes vacances', or, literally, 'the big holidays', and then the cycle starts again. What makes the academic year fascinating is the wealth of activities and incidents, planned or unplanned, that pepper the academic calendar. The unexpected and surprise elements make for added spice in the daily broth and school leaders have usually done enough rounds of this cycle to lead others through the navigation of the education seas. Experience pays off. Most, if not all, headteachers have walked a mile in the shoes of the class teacher and in some cases of the non-teaching staff member too, so they have honed their craft and can walk the walk, talk the talk and keep their integrity intact. I know for me this is certainly how I aim to be every day of my working life.

I love what I do. It's not always easy but there are equal measures of pleasure and pain – actually more pleasure than pain – as well as the benefits of the rewards which last a lifetime.

Walking the walk is one of several mantras I have held onto. Let me give you a few of the other mantras I have developed along my journey to headship:

Leave things better than I found them.

It's very similar to what the great New Zealand rugby team, the All Blacks, have as their mission statement which is to 'leave the jersey in a better place' and 'push past possible'.

#livetoleavealegacy

This is something I often decorate my social media with and, finally, *'Know your worth'.*

Useful links

Blogs with useful thoughts:

https://headteachersroundtable.wordpress.com

https://jillberry102.blog

https://johntomsett.com

https://itsthejourneynotdestination.wordpress.com

About the Author

Miriam   Manderson has over 28 years of teaching experience with inner-London schools and is headteacher of a large secondary school in Outer London. She was in her first year of headship when she began writing this book. The first year of headship had an abrupt and unusual academic interruption with the crisis presented by the Covid-19 pandemic. Who would ever have imagined navigating the sea of educational resources with this world event occurring? What better way of using the time than to share her experience of working her way up to becoming a headteacher in this book?

Miriam is also the creator of a journal for other leaders, The Conscious Leader's Thought Pad.

She is a remarkable headteacher, a mother of two boys, a wife, a sister, a stepmother to four, a step grandmother to eight, a godmother to three and an aunty to several.

Raised in the northwest area of London, characterised by high levels of deprivation and crime, arriving at headship has been a monumental achievement in her life, but still, she will modestly admit to not knowing it all, or even having the confidence you would expect. That keeps her humble.

Miriam has an insatiable appetite to reverse the effects of disadvantage as well as to enhance the development and command of the English language and literacy in young people, believing that this empowers them to have a voice in this world. She was a key contributor to the 'Look Like Me Book Challenge', an initiative that supported 30 children authors to write one collective community book, *The Popcorn House*, to help counteract the underrepresentation of children of Black and other 'minority' ethnicities in children's publications.

She lives with her husband and sons in London.

References

Berry, J. (2016). *Making the Leap: Moving from Deputy to Head.* Cornwall: Crown House Publishing.

Blackteachersconnect (2021). *Black teachers connect CIC.* Retrieved from blackteachersconnect.co.uk: https://blackteachersconnect.co.uk/

Blackteacherseducate! (2021). *Black Teachers Educate!* Retrieved from https://www.blackteacherseducate.com/

#blackteachersofinstagram (2021). *https://www.instagram.com/explore/tags/blackteacher sofinstagram/?hl=en-gb.* (Instagram)

Brown, B. (2018). *Dare to Lead. Brave Work. Tough Conversations. Whole Hearts.* London: Vermilion.

Bullock, M. P. H. (2019, October). *https://www.london.gov.uk/sites/default/files/adverse_ childhood_experiences_in_london._final_report_octobe r_2019_with_author._mb.pdf.* Retrieved from https://www.london.gov.uk/: https://www.london.gov.uk/sites/default/files/adverse _childhood_experiences_in_london._final_report_octo ber_2019_with_author._mb.pdf

Collins, J. (2001). *Good To Great: Why Some Companies Make the Leap … and Others Don't.* Random House Business.

ConvertUnits.com. (n.d.). *Days from date calculator.* Retrieved August 30, 2019, from ConvertUnits.com: https://www.convertunits.com/dates/100/daysfrom/M ay+24,+2019

Covey, S. R. (1989). *The 7 Habits of Highly Effective People: Powerful Lessons in Personal Change.* Bath: Simon & Schuster.

DfE (2021) *School teacher workforce*, Retrieved February 2021 from https://www.ethnicity-facts-figures.service.gov.uk/workforce-and-business/workforce-diversity/school-teacher-workforce/latest#by-ethnicity-and-gender-headteachers-only

Dave (2019). Black. Retrieved May 2020, from https://youtu.be/pDUPSNdmFew

Ehrmann, M. (1927). *Words for life*. Retrieved June 2020, from All Poetry: https://allpoetry.com/desiderata---words-for-life

Google (2021, May). *#I Am Remarkable*. Retrieved from https://iamremarkable.withgoogle.com/

Grant, V. (2014). *Staying A Head. The Stress Management Secrets of Successful School Leaders.* London: Integrity Coaching.

Hansen, M.V. a. o. (n.d.). *https://www.brainyquote.com/authors/mark-victor-hansen-quotes*. Retrieved from BrainyQuotes.com.

Ibarra, H., Carter, N. M. & Silva, C. (2010). *Why Men Still Get More Promotions Than Women*. Retrieved July 2021 from Harvard Business Review: https://hbr.org/2010/09/why-men-still-get-more-promotions-than-women

Korsch, A. (2011, June 23). *Suits.* USA.

Morgan, P. (2019). *The Crown*. 'Aberfan', episode three, season 3. Netflix. Retrieved 2019.

Paisley, B. (2010, January 1). *Twitter.com*. Retrieved from https://twitter.com/BradPaisley/status/7260619293?s= 20 .

Pierson, R. (2013, May). *Every Kid Needs a Champion*. Retrieved from TED Talks Education: https://www.ted.com/talks/rita_pierson_every_kid_ne eds_a_champion?language=en

Swainston. T. (2012). The 7 Cs of Leadership Success: Unlock Your Inner Potential And Become A Great Leader. AuthorHouse UK.

Syed, M. (2010). *Bounce, The Myth of Talent and the Power of Practice.* New York: Harper Collins.

The Key (n.d.). Retrieved from The Key for School Leaders: https://schoolleaders.thekeysupport.com/

UCL, IoE (2020, December 14). *46% of all schools in England have no BAME teachers.* Retrieved from https://www.ucl.ac.uk/: https://www.ucl.ac.uk/ioe/news/2020/dec/46-all-schools-england-have-no-bame-teachers

Walsh, S. (2008). *I'm Not Wonder Woman, But God Made Me Wonderful.* Thomas Nelson Books.

(Wikipedia, n.d.) https://en.wikipedia.org/wiki/Made_man#:~:text=To%20becom e%20%22made%22%2C%20an,silence%20and%20code%20of% 20honor

Williamson, M. (2015). *A Return to Love: Reflections on the Principles of 'A Course in Miracles'.* Harper Thorsons.